▼▼▼▼▼▼▼▼▼▼▼▼▼▼▼▼

HOW
TO SUCCEED
In
WRITTEN WORK
And
STUDY

▲▲▲▲▲▲▲ ▲▲▲▲▲▲▲▲▲▲

HOW TO SUCCEED IN WRITTEN WORK AND STUDY

RICHARD ELLIS AND
KONRAD HOPKINS
with cartoons by
CRAIG MACLACHLAN

COLLINS
London & Glasgow

First published 1985

© William Collins Sons and Company Limited
Printed in Great Britain by Collins Glasgow

ISBN 0 00 434283 6

Acknowledgements

We wish to express our gratitude and thanks to: Dr George Brown, University of Nottingham, for allowing us to use his POKEEARS system in the chapter on listening and note taking; Mr Ian Crofton, Collins Publishers, for his editorial guidance; Mr Dave Crombie for extracts from *The Complete Synthesizer* (published by Omnibus Press, London), reproduced with permission; Mr M. Cummings, Stevenson College of Further Education, Edinburgh, for his reading of some of the text and helpful suggestions; Mr David Dewar, Paisley College of Technology, for granting us permission to use his report, 'How an Electronic Music Synthesizer Works', in the chapter on report writing; Mr Gerald Donnelly, University of Glasgow, for his assistance in preparing the typescript of this book for publication; Professor Philip Hobsbaum, University of Glasgow, for his interest and sharing with us of his ideas and suggestions; Ms Flora Laverty, Senior Librarian, The Queen's College, Glasgow, for her suggestions on the section on libraries; Dr A. McClintock, The Queen's College, Glasgow, for her reading of some of the text and helpful suggestions; Professor J.F. Woodward, Paisley College of Technology, for his interest and encouragement; and our students, who have taught us much about the skills of effective writing, speaking, listening and reading.

R.E.
K.H.

Contents

CONTENTS

Introduction

A handbook is a reference work which can be easily handled and consulted. As such, this handbook is, in part, a guide to accepted practices and usages in language, writing essays, reports and letters, conducting research, giving short talks (sometimes with the use of audiovisual aids), and developing and extending reading and listening skills. It is also, in part, a 'how-to-do-it' book, in which we show by examples and figures how the practices work and what the usages are in different circumstances and contexts. This handbook is not meant to be read straight through, but dipped into when help or advice is needed in finding answers to questions and problems relating to written and/or spoken communication.

This handbook is designed to be used in conjunction with other reference works, such as the *Collins English Dictionary*, the *New Collins Thesaurus*, and bibliographies and catalogues which are found in most libraries. At the end of each chapter, we provide a summary box of main points for quick review, and suggest selected titles for further reading. To emphasize — and 'dramatize' — certain key points in the text, and to help you remember these points, each chapter is illustrated with a selection of cartoons (by Craig Maclachlan).

The intended readership of this handbook is primarily among students in higher and further education institutions, who are taking courses not only in the arts, business and the social sciences, but also in pure science and technology. In most cases, students are capable of communicating their ideas, knowledge, experiences, opinions and research findings well enough — perhaps very well. But almost everyone, no matter how accomplished in communicating with others, can benefit from help or advice in improving his or her communication skills.

Furthermore, prospective employers expect graduates or sandwich-course students seeking jobs to be able to write clearly and correctly and to speak confidently and intelligibly. These skills, together with the ability to listen attentively and read efficiently, are valuable assets for any job-seeker to possess.

Our practical aim in this handbook is, therefore, to offer students (and others too) the assistance and suggestions which, we believe, will make them more effective communicators and receivers of communications, whether in their academic environments or in their work places.

Although we are aware of the electronic communications revolution, and refer to examples of it in certain chapters, we concentrate on the traditional means of written and spoken communication. Despite the wide availability and application of computers, word processors and other electronic communications devices, most of us still communicate with one another by exchanging written and spoken words. Even messages composed on word processors, for instance, are texts constructed of words and sentences according to the rules and usages of English grammar, spelling and punctuation.

To illustrate the various points and ideas presented and discussed in this handbook, we have included sample letters and a talk outline, as well as an essay (on a language topic) and a report (on a technical topic). These texts serve as guides rather than as absolute models to follow, so do not hesitate to adapt them to your individual needs. It may be, however, that some students will be expected to use recommended departmental or institutional 'house styles' in preparing letters, essays, reports and talks. If this is the case, our guides will be useful mainly to those who have no other guides to follow.

Before considering the practical uses and applications of English in the several categories we have mentioned, we feel that it may be of interest to make a few observations about this language we speak and write.

English is the first language of some 500,000,000 people, worldwide, and the second or third language of many millions more. UNESCO reports that over 60% of the world's radio programmes and about 70% of all letters posted are in English. If any language can be called 'a world language', it is probably English.

A relatively young language, English has been growing, developing and changing for only about 1,500 years. It started as Anglo-Saxon, also known as Old English. To this core language of a few thousand words have been added words from Latin, Greek, Norse (as seen, for example, in the 'by' and 'thorpe' endings in certain place names on the east coast of England), French (following the Norman Conquest in 1066), and many other languages of the world.

From this mixture has emerged modern English, with a vocabulary of over 500,000 words. Besides borrowing words from other languages, English has also accepted neologisms (newly-minted words), such as 'micro chip', 'panda car' and 'hologram', into its vocabulary, while other words have passed out of usage or changed their meanings, e.g. 'gramophone', 'wireless' and 'valve'. In addition to changes in vocabulary, English grammar and spelling have often undergone striking changes too. These changes are immediately noticeable when you attempt to read Chaucer's Middle English in *The Canterbury Tales* or even Shakespeare's Elizabethan English. To read *Beowulf* (8th century A.D.) in the original, you must first learn Anglo-Saxon as you would a foreign language.

Ideas of what is 'correct' English have also changed considerably over the years, and still vary within the English-speaking community. Contrary to the opinions of some purists, there is no one and only 'correct' English. British English differs in some spellings, vocabulary and idioms from American English, for example:

U.K.   I have got a new tyre, windscreen and bonnet for my car, and I paid for them by cheque.

U.S.   I've gotten a new tire, windshield and hood for my automobile, and I paid for them with a check.

There are also variations in English forms and usages in Canada, Australia, New Zealand, South Africa, the Philippines (the third largest English-speaking country), and other countries where English is spoken. Within the U.K. itself, as within these other countries, variation in form and usage exist. Acceptable in these communities, the variations must be considered 'correct' for those who use them. Correctness is determined by usage, appropriateness and acceptability in the language area.

Standard English is, on the other hand, a concept associated more with written than spoken forms, because the 'standard' is more definitely established in spelling than in pronunciation. Standard English is the form of the language that draws least attention to itself throughout the English-speaking world, using the vocabulary, idioms, spelling, grammar and syntax which enables us to be readily understood in speech and writing, on a wide range of topics.

Richard Ellis
Konrad Hopkins

Further Reading

Foster, B.   *The Changing English Language*. Pelican, 1970.

Pei, M.   *The Story of English*. A Premier Book, 1962.

Potter, S.   *Our Language*, Revised Edition. Pelican, 1967.

Chapter 1   Words, Meanings, Contexts

Meanings and how they are determined

Of the 500,000 or so words in the *Oxford English Dictionary,* only about 5,000 are in everyday use. In another chapter, we consider the kinds of information about words, including meaning, which can be obtained from a dictionary, but for the purpose of this present chapter, we will focus only on their meanings and how these are determined.

Changing meanings

Meanings of words vary with the passage of time and changing social circumstances, and in different locales. Few words remain constant in their meanings. For instance, the meaning of the word 'nice' has undergone several changes since it entered English from the Latin *nescius* and meant 'ignorant'. Later it meant 'stupid or wanton', before becoming the modern 'agreeable, pleasant', while its alternative meaning of 'requiring precision, care, tact or discernment', as in a 'nice point' or a 'nice question', is less common today.

New meanings; obsolete, archaic words

New words are pouring into the language from a great variety of sources, such as science, technology, politics, the mass media, the pop, youth and drug cultures, etc. People used to listen to the 'wireless', which was replaced by the 'radio', which in turn also became known as a 'transistor' (often shortened to 'tranny'). Thanks to the microelectronic revolution, we have a new meaning for 'chip', as well as such neologisms (new words) as 'byte', 'word processor', and 'random access', among many others. Once upon a time 'gay' meant 'merry', and 'hooked' was something granny did to a rug or grandpa did to a fish. On the other hand, some words pass out of fashion, if not out of the language, and are labelled 'archaic' (antiquated, but still retained in a special Biblical or legal context, e.g. 'thine') or 'obsolete' (no longer used in everyday language, e.g. 'tramcar').

Words with same spellings, different meanings

One of the features of English is the number of words which have the same spellings but different meanings. For instance, the word 'chamber' has many meanings as a noun:

- a room, especially a bedroom
- a set of rooms in a larger building
- a judge's room
- one of the houses of Parliament
- an organization to develop trade and commerce

- enclosed space in the body of an animal or plant
- part of a gun bore, separate area in a gun or revolver
- an underground vault
- a burial place

If we use the word as an adjective, we have additional meanings, as in

- chamber music
- chamber pot

- chamber counsel
- chambermaid

This diversity of choice allows you to pick the words and the meanings you need.

Synonyms

In addition to the words having the same spellings but different meanings, there are many words with different spellings but similar if not the same meanings, called synonyms, for example, 'beauty', 'loveliness', 'comeliness', 'fairness', 'good looks', 'gorgeousness' and 'handsomeness'. To aid you in choosing the right word and in enriching your vocabulary, a useful tool is the *New Collins Thesaurus* a 'treasury' (the meaning of 'thesaurus') that lists synonyms under headwords arranged alphabetically as in a dictionary.

Words with similar sounds, different spellings/meanings

Another feature of English, which sometimes causes problems in spelling as well as understanding of meaning, is the number of words with similar sounds but different spellings and meanings. Among the problem words are these pairs which are sometimes confused:

- counsellor/councillor
- access/excess
- accept/except
- affect/effect

- affluent/effluent
- farther/father
- feet/feat

Denotative/connotative meanings

Words have two kinds of meaning: denotative and connotative. The denotation of a word is its dictionary definition or definitions. For example, the noun 'table' means — denotes — a piece of furniture; the noun 'bird' means — denotes — any member of a class (Aves) of warm-blooded vertebrates more or less completely covered with feathers (it has other meanings, too, such as a clay pigeon, a shuttlecock in badminton, and a hissing or jeering in disapproval).

Define words in their own terms

Note that words are defined in their own terms, that is, a noun is defined in terms of a noun (a person, place or thing), a verb in terms of a verb (action or state of being), and so on. For example, a 'table' (noun) is a piece (noun) of furniture. It is *not* a 'where' (adverb) as in 'a table is where you eat your meals' or a 'when' (adverb) as in 'a table is when your mum tells you to sit down and eat at it'.

Connotative meanings

Denotative meanings of words are relatively simple. Connotative meanings can be more difficult, because they are the suggested ideas or 'feelings' associated with words additional to their explicit dictionary meanings.

The difference between denotative and connotative meanings can be represented in this diagram, using, as an example, the word 'mother':

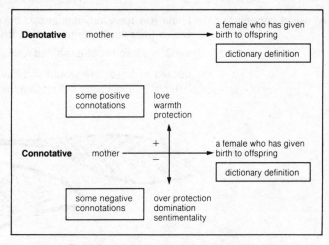

Fig. 1 Denotative and connotative meanings

Context

It is necessary for you to ensure that your reader grasps the meanings which you want him or her to grasp. One way to do so is by the context in which the words appear. You seldom write down words by themselves. You put them into phrases, clauses, sentences and paragraphs, which become essays, reports, letters and other texts. All these surrounding words are the context in which any given word appears, and contribute to determining the meaning or meanings of individual words. The word 'country', for example, although it has several possible meanings, will be placed in a context which will make the writer's intention clear. For example:

My country right or wrong.

I prefer country-and-western to rock-and-roll.

I'd like to live in the country.

Scotland is the country where Burns was born.

The country is going to the dogs.

Don't quote out of context

Context is sometimes vitally important in conveying the full meaning of a word or phrase. When a person complains that a journalist has quoted him or her 'out of context', that person is saying that the meaning of a statement has been distorted or misrepresented by being separated from the surrounding passage. It is, of course, essential that you keep the meaning of words, phrases and sentences intact when you are quoting from a source while researching a topic for an essay or a report.

Use of connotation in advertising

Some writers and speakers may use a word in such a way as to suggest several meanings. For instance, an advertiser of bicycles who announces:

> Our bikes, good for their balance, reassuring for yours

is using 'balance' both in the sense of equilibrium and of bank balance.

Poets' use of connotation

Poets, too, have long recognized the power of connotative meanings to enrich their verses. Suppose that Robert Burns had written

> O, my love is like a red, red ruby

instead of 'rose'. He would still have had the repetition of the initial letter 'r' (alliteration), but broken the metre and rhythm of the line, and

though 'ruby' has connotations of its own, they are not so suggestive of romance and love as 'rose'. Burns chose exactly the right word for his purpose, at the same time suggesting many amorous ideas and feelings for his readers to enjoy.

Uncertainty of meaning intended

No writer, however, can be sure how far readers will extend the associations of a word. For instance, when Captain Scott wrote of the South Pole:

> Great God, this is an awful place

did he intend his readers to understand 'awful' to mean 'full of awe, power, wonder', or the more modern equivalent of 'terrible, horrible', or both? As words change their meanings over the years, old connotations disappear and new ones arise.

Scientific/technical writing: objective, non-connotative

On the other hand, scientific and technical texts should be written as far as possible in an objective, precise, impersonal, and non-suggestive style, with words which have only one definite meaning. The writer of such texts wants to avoid connotations which may create ambiguity.

SUMMARY OF THE MAIN POINTS

- New words are entering the language, just as other words are becoming obsolete.

- Words have denotative (dictionary) and connotative (suggested) meanings.

- The context in which words appear also helps to determine their meanings.

- To avoid misusing a word, consult a dictionary to check its meaning or meanings.

Chapter 2   Ambiguity and Cliché

Ambiguity (from the Latin *ambigere*, both ways) is defined as an expression capable of having more than one meaning. One kind of ambiguity is intentional, another is accidental. Much of our humour is based on intentional ambiguity, often as a pun or play on words. For example:

> DOCTOR   Well, Mr Smith, you must give up smoking.
> PATIENT   You've said that before. I'd like a second opinion.
> DOCTOR   Very well then — you're a damn fool!

The ambiguity is in the patient's intended meaning of 'second opinion'.

But the accidental kind of ambiguity may not be funny at all. 'Advance to the front' was part of an order sent by the commander of the Light Brigade forces to his commander in the field. In this case, the word 'front' was dangerously ambiguous. Which was meant — the battle front or the direction in which to move? Many soldiers died because of the misunderstanding of this order.

Pronoun reference

Ambiguity sometimes arises from loose or imprecise pronoun reference, e.g. 'who', 'which', 'it', 'they', 'he'. You must make sure that the reader understands to what and/or to whom you are referring. For example:

> The faster the <u>test engineers</u> ran the motors, the hotter <u>they</u> became.

It is fairly clear that the 'they' refers to the motors, but it might possibly refer to the test engineers. There is a little doubt in this example, and even more in the next one:

> The faster the <u>test engineers</u> ran the <u>motors</u>, the more problems <u>they</u> encountered.

The writer could be referring to the motors developing problems as well as to the test engineers who faced increasing difficulties. Before the ambiguity can be eliminated, the writer must decide which meaning he or she wishes to convey, and rephrase the sentence accordingly.

A sentence in a student's economics essay ran thus:

> The <u>computer firms</u> had great hopes for their <u>new research efforts</u>, but <u>they</u> encountered severe financial difficulties.

Who or what has 'encountered severe financial difficulties', the firms or the efforts? The sentence might be rewritten as follows:

> The computer firms had great hopes for their new research efforts, but <u>these</u> encountered severe financial difficulties.

The ambiguity is thus removed.

The following example has more than one kind of ambiguity in it:

> The building workers examined sites for new houses.
> <u>They</u> overlooked the green belt.

One problem is 'they'. Does it refer to 'new houses' or 'building sites'? A second ambiguity is in the word 'overlooked', which can mean 'to see over something' or 'to forget to do something' or 'ignore'. Which does the writer mean? We can guess at his or her meaning, but only the writer will know for sure.

Adverb reference

Another cause of ambiguity in writing is adverb reference. For instance:

> The driving instructor only guessed at the real worries she had.

Was the driving instructor the only human being in the world to guess at what worried the lady? Or, did the driving instructor not really know, but could only guess at her worries? We can clear up the ambiguity by rewriting the sentence as:

> Only the driving instructor guessed at the real worries she had.

Consider the problem of meaning in this sentence:

> 'He didn't pass luckily' was the driving instructor's remark when he returned to the office.

Did the driving instructor mean that it was by luck that the candidate didn't pass his test? Or, did he mean that luckily for other drivers, the candidate failed his test? Probably the writer meant:

> 'Lucklily, he didn't pass . . .'

Take care in placing adverbs (such as 'only' and 'luckily') in a sentence. It helps to read the sentence aloud to yourself to test whether it means what you intend it to.

Faulty punctuation

Ambiguity can arise through faulty punctuation. Sometimes the results are amusing:

> She particularly ordered tea and rolls in bed.

> The car hit the tree moving as I was on thick ice there was no chance to stop.

The reason that some letters people write to insurance companies are funny is that an essential comma or full stop has been omitted from a sentence. The unfortunate motorist should have written:

> The car hit the tree. Moving as I was on thick ice, there was no chance to stop.

Then the facts of the accident would have been clearer. A sensible and sensitive use of punctuation will help you to avoid ambiguity in your writing.

Awkward linkage of words

The source of ambiguity may also be in the awkward linkage of words in a sentence or expression. Consider this advert:

> Piano for sale by private seller with oak veneer.

A comma after 'seller' would have somewhat reduced the nonsense, but it would be better to rewrite the advert:

> Piano with oak veneer for sale by private seller.

Now contemplate the picture this sentence conjures up:

The lady at the typewriter with a large hat was the one who broke the news to me.

The linkage of ideas — and image — is so muddled that inserting a few commas will not much help in clarifying the meaning. We can rewrite it as:

It was the lady with the large hat who sits at the typewriter who broke the news to me.

Or:

The news was broken to me by that lady with the large hat over there at the typewriter.

Clichés

A cliché is an over-used phrase or expression. It is a word which comes from the French *clicher*, to stereotype, a term from the printing trade. If you use phrases and expressions such as

without further ado	at this moment in time
at the drop of a hat	too many cooks spoil the broth
in this day and age	leave no stone unturned
well and truly	cutting off your nose to spite your face
all good men and true	by hook or by crook

By hook or by crook?

among hundreds of other similar well-worn expressions, you are using clichés, and you can't expect your readers or listeners to be much interested in what you are writing or saying.

Two groups of clichés

We can divide clichés into two groups. The first group consists of the idioms which have become so commonplace that they are unworthy of comment. Examples of this group are 'leave no stone unturned' and 'by hook or by crook'.

The second group is made up of quotations — and misquotations — from authors which have been so frequently cited that they have lost all their original relevance and freshness. Among the over-used quotations are 'To be or not to be' and 'A thing of beauty is a joy forever', and among the misquotations are 'A little knowledge [it's 'learning'] is a dangerous thing' and 'the best laid plans [it's 'schemes'] o' mice an' men'. Even certain lines from pop-song lyrics are becoming clichés through over quotation, such as, 'I'm all shook up', 'The times, they are a-changin', 'I can't get no satisfaction', and 'Bridge over troubled waters'. Advertisers and politicians, too, have created slogans which have become clichés: 'Keep death off the road', 'A Mars a day . . .', 'Things go better with Coke', 'Labour isn't working', and 'Britain's on the Right Track'.

Clichés are built into our modes of expression. It is difficult to avoid them altogether. People cannot be expected to be constantly minting new ways of expressing old ideas: after all, there's nothing new under the sun (another cliché). Without clichés, we would be more often than not (yet another cliché) hard put (still another cliché) to find a suitably striking substitute expression. The reason that certain clichés — such as 'cool as a cucumber', 'every Tom, Dick and Harry', and 'let them eat

Cool as a cucumber.

cake' — are so often repeated is that they are excellent expressions which serve their purpose very well. Somehow, such substitutes as 'cool as a carrot', 'every Jimmy, George and Charlie' and 'let them eat scones' don't quite measure up to the familiar, tried and tested (yes, another cliché) clichés.

Avoid clichés

If you can devise a new and interesting way of expressing an old idea, good for you. But perhaps the best advice is to try to avoid using the stalest phrases and most often repeated quotations (or misquotations). Writing, to be effective, must capture and sustain your reader's interest, and you will not do so by clothing your ideas in trite phrases and hackneyed expressions. To quote from Proverbs 25:1, which is a seldom cited Biblical passage:

A word fitly spoken is like apples of gold in pictures of silver.

SUMMARY OF THE MAIN POINTS

- Ambiguity usually arises from loose pronoun or adverb reference, faulty punctuation and awkward linkage of words.

- Clichés are over-used phrases and quotations (or misquotations) and should be avoided.

Chapter 3

Grammar: Words into Sentences

What is grammar?

The word 'grammar' comes from the Greek word *gramma*, letter, which derives from the Greek word *graphein*, to write. Thus grammar can be defined as 'the science of letters or writing'. It deals with the classes of words, their changes of form (inflections) to mark distinctions of case:

his book   their books

of gender:

her song   his song

of number:

house   houses

of person:

I come.   He comes.

of tense:

I come.   I came.   I will come.

of mood:

if I were you

of voice:

I open the door.   The door was opened by me.
active   passive

Grammar also shows the mutual relations and functions of words in a sentence according to accepted usage (syntax).

Good grammar is correct usage

A belief held by some language authorities is that each language, English included, has a 'pure' or 'grammatical' form which is always 'correct' and which exists independently of usage. Another belief held by these authorities is that local dialects are not 'real English', that somewhere there is a perfect standard language removed from time, place, and the people who use it.

Both these beliefs are wrong. The sole standard for language is and always has been that of current usage. As one authority on English grammar has written, 'The first object in studying grammar is to learn to observe linguistic facts as they *are*, not as they *ought* to be, or as they were in an earlier stage of the language.'

Grammar, the rules of language usage

Grammar concerns all the rules of language usage. It classifies words into all sorts of categories and describes the peculiarities of each category. To do so efficiently, grammar has as many categories as are

17

required, and designates each category by a term which enables us to recognize it.

So, first, let's define some of the basic grammatical categories and terms:

Parts of speech

I. **Parts of speech,** which are the different kinds of words used for different purposes in a sentence:

1. Noun: a word used to name a person, place, thing, feeling, idea, etc. The word 'noun' is from the Latin *nomen,* a name.

We can divide nouns into:

proper nouns (people and places which take capitals), e.g.:

Mr Jones   Bill   London   Rhine

collective nouns (groups), e.g.:

herds   flocks   school   shoal

common nouns, e.g.:

air   mountain   dust   jam

abstract nouns, e.g.:

fear   joy   honour   death   sorrow

2. Pronoun: a word used instead of a noun (from the Latin *pro,* for, instead of), e.g.:

I   you   he   she   it

A pronoun is a substitute word or proxy, denoting a person, place or thing without naming it. See IV below for particulars on the different kinds of pronouns.

3. Adjective: a word used to enlarge the meaning and narrow the application of a noun, i.e. a word that qualifies (modifies) a noun. The word 'adjective', from the Latin *adjectivus,* means 'used for adding on'.

Included among adjectives are the definite article 'the', and the indefinite articles 'a' and 'an'.

Adjectives can be compared in these degrees:

positive:

bad   good

comparative:

worse   better

superlative:

worst   best

Sometimes the comparative and superlative degrees are created by placing 'less' or 'more', and 'least' or 'most', in front of the adjective.

4. Verb: a word used for saying something about something else, denoting an action or state of being or feeling. 'Verb' is from the Latin *verbum,* a word, and is usually regarded as the chief word in a sentence and the most important kind of word in human speech. See III below for more particulars on the verb.

5. Preposition: a word used to show or define the relationship that one thing has to another. The noun or noun-equivalent that comes after a preposition is called its 'object', and the preposition is said to 'govern' the noun or noun-equivalent, e.g.:

<u>up</u>   hill   and   <u>down</u>   dale
prep noun   prep   noun

6. Conjunction: a word used to connect words or groups of words, and showing a relationship between the words or groups, e.g.:

He came <u>and</u> conquered.

He came <u>but</u> vanished.

He came <u>because</u> of you.

He came <u>therefore</u> I saw what he had to offer.

7. Adverb: a word used to extend the meaning and restrict the application of any part of speech except a noun or noun-equivalent. In English, many adverbs are identified by the '-ly' ending of the word.

Like adjectives, adverbs can be compared in degrees:

positive: early
comparative: earlier
superlative: earliest

as well as with the use of 'less' or 'more' and 'least' or 'most' for the comparative and superlative degrees respectively.

8. Interjection: a word used to express emotion, such as 'oh', 'ah', and 'alas', but forming no part of the structure of the sentence. The word 'interjection' is from the Latin *interjectus*, thrown between. Being absolute and isolated in the sentence, it cannot be qualified by any other word.

Four kinds of words: two parts of speech in one

II. In addition to the eight parts of speech defined above, there are four kinds of words that are two parts of speech combined in one:

1. Participle: a verb and an adjective combined; also called a verbal adjective, e.g.:

The <u>retired</u> teacher gave out the prizes.

The word 'retired' is part of the verb 'to retire', and it is also an adjective, modifying the word 'teacher'.

2. Gerund: a verb and a noun combined; also called a verbal noun, e.g.:

She is thinking of <u>retiring</u> from her job.

The word 'retiring' is part of the verb 'to retire', and it is also a noun, the object of the preposition 'of'.

3. Infinitive: also a verb and a noun combined, e.g.:

He wishes <u>to return</u> the money.

Here 'to return' is the infinitive form of the verb, but, as the object of the transitive verb 'wish', it is also a kind of noun.

4. Relative adverb: partly an adverb and partly a conjunction; also called a conjunctive adverb, e.g.:

I was relieved <u>when</u> the exam ended.

Here 'when', modifying the verb 'was', is an adverb, but because it joins 'I was relieved' and 'the exam was over', it is also a conjunction.

About the verb   **III.** Here are a few facts about the verb:

1. Any part of a verb which can be used to say something about something else is called **finite**, which means 'limited', because it is limited to the same person (first, second, or third) or to the same number (singular or plural), e.g.:

He hit the ball.

2. Those parts of a verb which are not limited to person or number, that is, are not finite, are of three kinds: infinitive, participle, and gerund.
a. Infinitive: in modern English, this form of the verb is usually preceded by the preposition 'to', except after auxiliary verbs (see III. 4) showing mood (e.g. 'can', 'may') and some other verbs, such as 'let', 'dare', and 'make'.
b. Participle: the English verb has two participles, the present, ending in '-ing', as in 'writing', and the past, usually ending in '-ed', '-d', '-t', '-en', or '-n', as in 'posted', 'wept', 'written'.
The participle is the adjectival form of the verb, which modifies a noun and also takes objects and qualifiers like a verb, e.g.:

Quickly shutting the book, he left the library.

c. Gerund: a verb used as a noun. See II, 2 above.

3. Verbs are either **transitive** or **intransitive**. A verb that requires an object to complete its meaning is called transitive (from the Latin for 'passing over' or 'passing on'), e.g.:

Ships <u>sail</u> the seas.
     verb   object

He <u>shot</u> a bird.
   verb object

ABOUT THE VERB

Some verbs make a complete sense by themselves, and these are called intransitive, e.g.:

Birds <u>fly</u>.   Winds <u>blow</u>.   Men <u>die</u>.

Many verbs can be both transitive and intransitive depending on the context.

4. Another kind of verb is called **auxiliary**, such as 'have', 'be', 'may', 'do', 'shall', 'will', 'can', 'must'. Auxiliary verbs help to form the tenses, voices and moods of other verbs (see III, 5-7 below).

5. Two other terms associated with the verb are tense and conjugation.
a. Tense (from Old French *tens*, from the Latin *tempus*, time, tense) is an inflectional form of a verb for the expression of distinctions of time. In English, there are three simple tenses:

present, e.g.:   I come.
past, e.g.:   I came.
future, e.g.:   I will come.

and three compound tenses:

present perfect, e.g.: I have come.
past perfect, e.g.:   I had come.
future perfect, e.g.: I will have come.

The principle parts of a verb are given as present, past, and past participle, for example, 'do', 'did', 'done', the past participle 'done' being the part that combines with the auxiliary verbs 'have' and 'will' to form the compound tenses, e.g.:

I do have a fear of flying.

I did have a fear of flying.

b. Conjugation (from the Latin *conjugare*, to join together) means in grammar 'derived from the same root', and refers to the inflection of verbs in voice, mood, tense, number and person.

6. The verb has two voices: **active** and **passive**. The active voice is the form of the verb that shows that the person or thing named by the subject of the sentence is performing the action, e.g.:

Tom <u>kicked</u> the ball.
subject verb   object

Here 'Tom' is the subject who performed the action of kicking the ball, so the form of the verb is in the active voice, past tense.

In the passive voice, the form of the verb shows that the person or thing named in the sentence is receiving the action, e.g.:

The ball <u>was kicked</u> by Tom.
subject   verb

Here 'ball' is the subject of the sentence, receiving the action of being kicked, so the form of the verb is passive voice, past tense.

7. Mood means the 'mode' or 'manner' in which a verb expresses itself. The three main moods for English verbs are indicative, imperative, and subjunctive.
a. The **indicative mood** states a fact or asks a question, e.g.:

The shop is closed.

Is the shop closed?

b. The **imperative mood** expresses a command or a polite request, e.g.:

Shut the window!

Shut the window, please.

In both cases, the 'you' is understood.

c. The **subjunctive mood** expresses a state, event, or act as possible, conditional, or wished for. It is seldom found in modern English usage, except in such expressions as

if I were you

far be it for me

or in such conditional statements as

If I were a rich man, I would buy a mansion.

Usually, the indicative mood is sufficient to suggest the doubt or possibility originally expressed by the subjunctive, but if it is not, then the use of 'should' or 'may' will serve the same purpose.

Terms associated with nouns and pronouns

IV. Nouns and pronouns also have terms associated with them, such as person, number and case.

1. Person: among personal pronouns we can differentiate between person. The person speaking is the first person:

I	me	(singular)
we	us	(plural)

The person spoken to is the second person:

you   (singular and plural)

The person spoken about is the third person:

it	him	her	he	she	(singular)
they	them				(plural)

We should remember that verbs inflect according to person, e.g.:
I come.   He com<u>es</u>.

2. Number: this refers to singular and plural, as indicated above.

3. Case: this is the form of the noun, pronoun, or adjective which expresses its relation to other words in the sentence. The three main cases in English are:

a. Nominative: the subject of any verb, e.g.:

I hit the ball.

In pronouns, the nominative case is indicated by the following inflections:

singular	plural
I	we
you	you
he she it	they
who	who

b. Objective (also called accusative): the direct object of an active verb or a preposition, that is, the person or thing directly affected by the action, e.g.:

I hit the <u>ball</u>.

In pronouns, the objective case is indicated by the following inflections:

singular	plural
me	us
you	you
him her it	them
whom	whom

c. Possessive (also called genitive): a noun or a pronoun that indicates possession or ownership. In pronouns, the possessive case is indicated by the following inflections:

singular	plural
my mine	our ours
your yours	your yours
his her hers its	their theirs
whose	whose

In nouns, the possessive case is indicated by adding 's (singular) or s' (plural), e.g.:

the girl'<u>s</u> dress   the girls<u>'</u> dresses

(Good usage restricts this form to nouns naming living things.) The possessive case is also formed by *of*-plus-noun, e.g.:

the rays <u>of</u> the sun

or by *of*-plus-relative-pronoun, e.g.:

the car the axle <u>of which</u> is broken

Other kinds of pronouns V. Apart from the personal and possessive pronouns, there are several other kinds of pronouns that are important to know.

1. Demonstrative pronouns: these point to the person or thing referred to:

this   these   that   those
such   the   other   the same

E.g.:

<u>These</u> are the jeans I want, not <u>those</u>.

2. Relative pronouns: these express a relationship to an antecedent and introduce a subordinate clause:

who   whom   which   that

E.g.:

relative pronoun
He knew only one <u>student</u> at the college <u>who</u> qualified for the job.
antecedent   subordinate clause

3. Interrogative pronouns: these ask a question:

who? which? what? whom? whose?

E.g.:

Who is coming to dinner?

What is your name?

4. Reflexive pronouns: these serve as the object of a reflexive verb:

myself   yourself   himself   herself
itself   ourselves   yourselves   themselves

E.g.:

The girls enjoyed themselves at the party.

5. Emphatic pronouns: these are reflexive pronouns used for emphasis, e.g.:

She herself cleaned the flat.

6. Indefinite pronoun: these refer in general to an unspecified number of persons or things:

any   one   anyone   anybody   nobody   nothing   something

E.g.:

Is anybody there?
Nobody answered.

7. Distributive pronouns: these refer to persons or things individually:

both   each   every   either   neither   none   all

E.g.:

Both ordered the book, but neither bought it.

Phrases, clauses, sentences

VI. The words of these parts of speech are the building blocks from which we construct phrases, clauses, and sentences, and now we will consider briefly what these word structures and their functions are.

1. Phrases: a phrase is intermediate between a single word and a sentence, is a group of words in which no finite verb is either expressed or understood. A phrase has the following functions:

   a. As a noun:

How to do this is an intriguing question.

   b. As an adjective:

A bird in the hand is worth two [birds] in the bush.

   c. As an adverb:

He waited a few hours.

   d. As a preposition:

She went on board the train.

   e. As a conjunction:

In case the house burns down, we have insurance.

f. As an interjection:

What a pity!

g. The participial phrase deserves special mention. The participle, whether present or past, functions as an adjective as well as a verb, and so the participial phrase modifies a noun or a noun-equivalent in a sentence, E.g.:

Entering the room, she saw her friends.
present
participle

Broken in half, the pencil was useless.
past
participle

Another kind of participial phrase is the absolute phrase, which stands free of any agreement with other parts of the sentence, e.g.:

The weather being good, we went to the park.

Here the noun ('weather') that the participle ('being good') modifies is included in the phrase itself.

2. Clauses: a clause, like a phrase, is a group of words that can function as a part of speech, but, unlike a phrase, has a subject and a verb (or predicate, i.e., that which asserts something). It may be a main (or independent) clause, a coordinate clause, or a subordinate (or dependent) clause.

a. A main clause stands on its own and does not depend on any other clause to convey its full meaning, e.g.:

I saw him.

b. Coordinate clauses are two or more main clauses joined by coordinating conjunctions, such as 'and', 'but', 'or', 'nor', 'for', e.g.:

I went to the room, and I opened the door.
main clause   main clause

c. A subordinate clause is one which is dependent on another and functions as a noun, an adjective or an adverb in a sentence, e.g.:

I saw him, but he didn't see me.
subordinate clause

3. Sentences: when your mind becomes aware of a single person, thing, or quality, such as 'mother', 'book', 'music', 'wealth', the result is called a notion, and it is expressed by a single word or phrase. When your mind compares two notions and joins them by a finite verb, the result is called a thought, and it is expressed by a sentence, a word that comes from the Latin *sententia*, a thought.

A sentence is a group of words, containing a subject (noun or noun-equivalent) and a verb (action or state of being), in which something is expressed about something else. It is the equivalent in words of the complete thought from your mind, and with sentences (complete thoughts) we compose paragraphs, from which we construct reports, essays, memos, letters, books, and so on.

Sentences may be classified according to their purposes:

a. To make a statement, assertion or declaration, e.g.:

He is a man.   It is raining.

NOTION
+
FINITE VERB
+
NOTION
=
SENTENCE/ THOUGHT

b. To ask a question, e.g.:

What time is it?

c. To issue commands, e.g.:

Go now.

d. To utter exclamations, e.g.:

If only it would stop snowing!

e. To offer greetings and other expressions which have no definite forms, e.g.:

Good evening.   Many happy returns.

Sentences may be also classified according to their structure, which is determined by the kind and number of clauses in them. We would advise you to restrict yourself for the most part to the following two kinds:

a. The simple sentence has only one clause, a main clause, consisting of one subject and one verb (predicate), e.g.:

The big man kicked the ball.

b. The complex sentence has one main clause together with one or more subordinate clauses, e.g.:

The big man kicked the ball <u>which collapsed into hundreds of pieces.</u>
subordinate clause

SUMMARY OF THE MAIN POINTS

■ Grammar, the science of letters or writing, deals with the classes of words, their changes in form (inflections), and mutual relations and functions of words according to accepted usage (syntax).

■ There are eight parts of speech: noun, pronoun, adjective, verb, preposition, conjunction, adverb, interjection.

■ Tense (time), mood (manner of expression) and voice (active and passive) are associated with the use of the verb.

■ Person, number and case are associated with the uses of nouns and pronouns.

■ Words can be combined into phrases, clauses (independent and subordinate), and sentences (preferably simple and/or complex).

■ A sentence is a statement that contains both a subject (noun or noun substitute) and a verb (also called a predicate), which indicates action or state of being.

Further Reading

Evans, H.	*Editing and Design, Book 1:* *Newsman's English.* Heinemann, 1972.
Palmer, S.	*Grammar.* Penguin, 1971.
Pink, M.A. and S.E. Thomas.	*English Grammar, Composition and* *Correspondence.* The Donnington Press, Cassell & Co., 1963.

Chapter 4 Sentences

Sentence unity

Consisting of a subject and a verb, a sentence is a unit of expression. A good sentence should have unity, that is, it must express one main idea. Although it may contain more than one fact, all the facts must relate to the main idea. Consider this sentence:

> The members of the youth club were all dressed in the latest fashions, and many of them are unemployed.

The first clause tells us about the members' clothing, while the second one mentions unemployment. The sentence does not have unity. The two different ideas don't belong together in one sentence, but should be stated in two separate sentences.

Loose and periodic sentences

The two types of sentences are loose and periodic, so called according to the arrangement of their parts. In a loose sentence, the main statement appears first and the qualifying phrases or clauses come after it, e.g.:

> Janice had been preparing herself to start her secretarial job with the director of the firm by practising her typing and increasing her shorthand speed.

In a periodic sentence, the qualifying phrases or clauses are stated first, and the main statement is put at the end, e.g.:

> By practising her typing and increasing her shorthand speed, Janice had been preparing herself to start her secretarial job with the director of the firm.

Emphasis in a sentence

It is sometimes necessary to emphasize a particular word or phrase in a sentence in order to sharpen the point or idea of the sentence. This emphasis may be achieved in several ways:

1. Repetition of certain words or phrases, e.g.:

> The dog was his only friend, his only companion, his only confidant, and his only heir.

The repetition of 'his only' stresses the uniqueness of the dog in this person's life. But the device of repetition can easily become boring, so use it sparingly.

2. Correlative conjunctions: these are conjunctions used in pairs, such as 'not only . . . but also' and 'rather . . . than', e.g.:

> She insisted that she wanted the pupils <u>not only</u> to read the poem, <u>but also</u> to memorize it.

> Tom considered the job he got <u>rather</u> as a piece of good luck <u>than</u> as a reward for excellence.

3. 'It is' and 'It was' constructions: these can emphasize an idea or a part of a sentence, e.g.:

> My sister sang the song very beautifully.

This might be reconstructed to place emphasis on 'my sister', as:

> <u>It was</u> my sister who sang the song very beautifully.

4. Parallel structure: this involves giving two or more parts of a sentence a similar form to point up a thought, e.g.:

> It is not <u>by providing</u> students with <u>a strict code of conduct,</u> but <u>by providing</u> them with <u>a good example of behaviour,</u> that the teacher maintains discipline in the classroom.

The words 'by providing' are used in both parts of the sentence, and the phrases 'a strict code of conduct' and 'a good example of behaviour' are parallel in structure and thought.

5. Antithesis and balance: related to parallel structure is antithesis, which is used to achieve balance in a sentence. In antithesis, opposites are balanced to produce an effective contrast, e.g.:

> People who never study the <u>past</u> will never understand the <u>present</u>.

6. Altering word order: this involves altering the natural order of certain words or phrases in a sentence and placing them where they will have more striking effect, e.g.:

> <u>Poor</u> though he was, he still gave money to charity.

The natural order would be 'Though he was poor . . .', but by inverting the order of subject and object, the fact that the man was 'poor' is emphasized. Here is another example:

> It is difficult to realize that he had composed two large orchestral works, three piano sonatas and two operas, all of them performed, and all of them successes, <u>by the time he was only fifteen years of age.</u>

Normally, 'by the time he was only fifteen years of age' would go after 'that', but by placing the phrase at the end of the sentence, the composer's youthfulness receives special attention and emphasis.

Variety in sentence structure

A sentence may be constructed in a variety of forms, as the examples of ways of obtaining emphasis show. A single sentence may be written with different structures without changing its meaning, e.g.:

> The disco was long and lively, and the students went home early in the morning.

can be recast as follows:

> After a long and lively disco, the students went home early in the morning.

> The students had a long and lively disco, and went home early in the morning.

> Having had a long and lively disco, the students went home early in the morning.

Single sentences in longer texts

A single sentence may also be a unit in a longer text, such as a paragraph, that comes before and after it. A series of short, simple sentences, or longer sentences all constructed in the same form, will soon become boring. Both short and long sentences have their uses, but in most student writing, variety in the length and the structure of the sentences contribute to making them more interesting and stimulating to read.

SUMMARY OF THE MAIN POINTS

■ A good sentence has unity, that is, it expresses one main idea, with a subject and a verb.

■ The two types of sentences are loose (main statement first, qualifiers after it) and periodic (qualifiers first, main statement last).

■ Emphasis in a sentence can be obtained by repetition, correlative conjunctions, 'it is/it was' constructions, parallel construction, antithesis/balance, and altering word order.

■ Variety in sentence structure introduces interest into your writing.

SENTENCES

Further Reading

Barrass, R.   *Scientists Must Write.*
                 Chapman and Hall, 1978.

Barrass, R   *Students Must Write.*
                 Methuen, 1982.

Evans, H.   *Editing and Design, Book 1:*
                 Newsman's English.
                 Heinemann, 1972.

Chapter 5   **Paragraphs**

What is a paragraph?

A paragraph is a group of sentences expressing one idea, complete in one section of writing or print. The rules for constructing a paragraph are similar to those for constructing a sentence.

Unity

A paragraph must have unity of idea, with all the sentences in it contributing to the development of the main topic. In a well constructed paragraph, the topic can be stated in a sentence. This is the topic sentence, and it may appear at either the beginning or at the end of the paragraph.

Topic sentence

If the topic sentence comes at the beginning, it will be followed by other sentences expanding on it or illustrating it with additional information. If the topic sentence comes at the end, it will serve as the climax of the preceding sentences which prepared for it. In most paragraphs, the topic sentence is found at the beginning because in this position it at once tells the reader what the idea or theme of the text is, thus holding his or her interest.

Topic sentence at the beginning

Here is an example of a paragraph with the topic sentence at the beginning:

> <u>Almost everyone in my family has a hobby.</u> My mother knits cardigans which she sometimes sells at charity functions. My father is interested in collecting stamps, but only from Great Britain. I have an aunt who has a camera with which she takes pictures of places she visits on her holidays abroad, and her son, my cousin, develops the prints for her in his lab, as photography is also his hobby. I myself have a fine assortment of fossils I've found on local hillsides. The only person in my family who doesn't have a hobby is my other aunt. She claims that hobbies are a waste of time.

The first sentence states the topic of the paragraph, which is about hobbies in one family. The following sentences elaborate the topic with details of the hobbies pursued by different members of the family, including the writer of the paragraph. The 'almost' in the topic sentence is justified by the fact that the second aunt has no hobby.

Coherence

A good paragraph should have coherence. The subject matter should be arranged in logical sequence, which should progress easily by the use of such transition connectives as 'however', 'moreover', 'furthermore', 'again', 'on the other hand', 'in conclusion', and the like. Consider the use of connectives in the following example:

> <u>Many are the moods of the sea.</u> Nothing is more awesome than a great storm, with mountainous waves, fiercely howling winds, and black clouds split by forks of lightning. <u>On the other hand,</u> on a fair, clear day, the surface of the sea rolls smoothly under a gentle

breeze. Or, again, a change for even better weather may result in a complete calm, not a breath of air stirring, and the sea as smooth as glass. However, this may be the calm before another storm, which may be a hurricane or even a typhoon, in which the sea is like a titanic monster raised from the ocean floor and attacking coasts with tidal waves and 100-mile-an-hour gales.

The topic sentence stands first, and all the succeeding sentences give instances of the many moods of the sea, using such connectives as 'on the other hand', 'or, again', and 'however' to link up the illustrations and indicate distinctions and contrasts.

Topic sentence at end

In the following paragraph, the topic sentence is placed at the end:

When you turn on your radio and tune in to the music stations, you might hear the top 40 hit songs. On another programme, however, you can listen to middle-of-the-road music, the standards and the golden oldies. But folk music is also featured on still other programmes, as are jazz, symphonies, church music, and operas. It's safe to say that there is considerable variety in the music offered on the music stations.

In this case, the last sentence summarizes the point of the paragraph: that radio music is varied. This topic sentence might have been placed at the beginning of the paragraph, but sometimes the sentence will have greater impact when placed last.

Implied topic sentence

Occasionally, a topic sentence is not explicitly stated but implied in the content of the paragraph, as in this example:

She washed and scraped the carrots, then diced them into the pot of water, seasoning them with a little salt. Switching on the hot plate, she placed the pot on the burner. In a few minutes, the water was boiling, and a few minutes after that the carrots were cooked. She drained off the water, placed the carrots in a dish, added butter, and ate the vegetables for her lunch.

There is no stated topic sentence, but the theme or idea here is preparing and cooking carrots for lunch, which is implied in the description of the procedure.

Emphasis by placing topic sentence

To heighten a point in a paragraph, it may be necessary to use one or more of the devices of emphasis. The placing of the topic sentence is a way of drawing the reader's attention to your idea. Placed at the beginning, the topic sentence can be developed in the remainder of the paragraph. Placed at the end, it can serve as the fitting conclusion to a chain of related ideas or facts. It may even be placed in the middle of the paragraph to show a certain balance in the material that comes before and after it.

Repetition for emphasis

It may be effective, too, to use repetition for the sake of emphasis in constructing a paragraph, but this device must not be overdone.

Parallel structure

The use of parallel structure may give additional force to a paragraph, but again there is a danger in overdoing the technique or in carrying it to extremes. Here is an example of the device of parallel structure used moderately to emphasize a point:

> He made a fortune by applying modern technology and imagination to selling the product. He was not the first to manufacture the product. He was not the first to market it. But he was the first to mass produce it. And he was the first to sell it to a mass audience by using clever advertising. In this way he made a million dollars before he was twenty-five.

Length of paragraph

The length of a paragraph is determined by what you have to say in it. One kind of topic may be fully developed in six or seven short sentences; another may require a dozen longer, more complicated sentences. You are advised not to attempt very long paragraphs because you might easily lose the thread of the topic in all the wordage. Nor should you produce nothing but a sequence of short, staccato paragraphs, which might become monotonous to the reader even if they are grammatically correct and clear. In practice, let the topic and its development, with facts, examples and qualifications, guide you in deciding the length of the paragraphs you write.

Readability

Whether your paragraphs are long or short, an important question to ask about them is: are they readable? Some texts are easier to read than others. The reason may be that the topic is interesting; or that the sentences are clear, correct, coherent and concise; or that the vocabulary is readily understandable; or all of these reasons. It may be, however, that in spite of good grammar and syntax, a text is still slow and heavy going, as if you were struggling through a thick fog to read it. Consider the readability of this passage of 100 words:

> It is a pernicious assumption on the part of dilettantish and unprofessional writers that their insipid, egregious and ineffectual drivelings are to be honoured by critics who have honed their scalpels on the lucubrations of masters past and present. The very opposite is true, for the critics, although they themselves may be incapable of concocting even the most contemptible effusions, take sadistic delight in decimating the villainous, insolent upstarts of the multiform literary arts. The critics find these scribblers abhorrent, and these scribblers return the compliment to the critics, whom they find unintelligent and pusillanimous as well as abhorrent.

The Fog Index

To calculate the Fog Index (F.I.) of this or any other passage, follow these steps:

1. take a sample passage of about 100 words

2. count the number of words in the sentences

3. divide the number of words in the passage by the number of sentences, giving the average length of sentence in the passage

4. count the number of words of three or more syllables in the passage (not counting proper names, compound words such as 'book-keeper' or verb forms such as 'created')

5. total the two factors just counted and multiply by 0.4 to obtain the Fog Index.

For the passage above:

1. number of words in sentence = 40, 35, 25

2. number of words in passage = 100

3. number of sentences = 3

4. average sentence length = 33.3 words

5. number of words of three or more syllables = 16 (16%)

6. average sentence length and percentage of words of three or more syllables added together = 33.3 + 16 = 49.3

7. 49.3 × 0.4 = a Fog Index of 19.72

High Fog Index

Readability level

Using the Fog Index system (derived from R. Gunning, *The Technique of Clear Writing*), make a check of your own writing to see whether it is becoming too difficult to read. If you are getting F.I. scores of over 13, you are approaching the danger level of reading difficulty, as in the passage quoted above with an F.I. of 19.72. The reader is likely to see more fog than sense in your writing. To decrease your Fog Index and increase your readability level, you might consider

• simplifying your sentence structure

• using shorter words

• being more concise

Concise rewrite

The text above might be rewritten in a more concise form (73 words), with a simpler vocabulary, and four rather than three sentences, thus considerably reducing the Fog Index, as follows:

Unprofessional writers assume that their bad or silly works will be honoured by critics who have sharpened their scalpels on the works of masters past and present. The reverse is true. The critics, although they may be unable to produce even poor works themselves, take cruel delight in cutting down the vile, cheeky amateurs. The critics hate these scribblers, and these scribblers regard the critics as stupid and cowardly as well as hateful.

SUMMARY OF THE MAIN POINTS

■ A paragraph is a group of sentences expressing one idea (unity).

■ A topic sentence, stating the theme or idea of a paragraph, can come at the beginning or at the end, or it may be implied in the subject matter.

■ A good paragraph should have coherence, with subject matter organized in a logical sequence.

■ Emphasis in a paragraph can be obtained by placement of topic sentence, repetition, and parallel structure.

■ Readability is determined mainly by the type of vocabulary used, the length of the sentences, and the conciseness of expression.

■ The Fog Index is a means of testing the readability of a piece of writing.

Further Reading

Barrass, R.   *Scientists Must Write,*
                 Chapman and Hall, 1978.

Gunning, R.   *The Technique of Clear Writing.*
                 McGraw-Hill, 1968.

Chapter 6   Punctuation, Capitals, Italics

Punctuation means 'pointing a text'

Punctuation (from the Latin *punctus*, point) is a set of marks or points used to separate the written language into sentences and parts of sentences. It is vital for making the writer's meaning clear, and essential if the reader is to make sense of the text. It corresponds to the inflections, stresses, pauses and rhythms of the human voice in speech.

The punctuation within a sentence is a guide to the structure of the sentence and the relationships of its various parts. It is a guide principally for the reader, who understands the meaning of the text through the eye, the act of reading being primarily a visual experience.

Punctuate for the silent reader

The writer punctuates for the convenience of the silent reader. Before the reader can understand the meaning of the text he or she must:

- grasp the structure of the sentence
- know where the construction begins and ends
- be able to distinguish minor constructions from major ones, and 'see' their proper relationships
- not run words together in such a way as to misunderstand their meanings

Good punctuation cannot compensate for loose sentence structure or careless use of language, but faults of punctuation can result in ambiguous statements, which are sometimes unintentionally funny, e.g.:

By tightening that large nut the engineer completed the task.

Common acceptance of punctuation

Although the invention of the printing press helped the principles of punctuation gain a certain amount of acceptance among writers and readers, these principles were not and are not hard and fast laws. Like language itself, punctuation has undergone changes over the years. Punctuation today is, generally, more sparingly used than it was in the past.

Experts disagree

Experts disagree on some procedures, and good authors will depart from most of the conventions of punctuation at one time or another to create special effects. Nevertheless, you will be able to learn more about punctuation from a careful consideration of a page of printed text than from any other source. One of the aims of this section is to help you to look more closely at what writers do with punctuation so that you can develop your own skills in handling the 'points'.

Close and open punctuation

Punctuation is called 'close' when the marks, especially commas, are used freely to mark the grouping or separation of words, phrases and clauses. It is called 'open' when the marks are omitted wherever possible without ambiguity.

Excessively close punctuation

There follows a practical guide to twelve main marks of punctuation, with examples to illustrate their conventional usage. The exceptions are also noted, along with information on the uses of capitals and italics (the latter represented on handwritten and typed texts by underlining).

The full stop ▪

The full stop is used:

1. at the end of a sentence, or any expression standing for a sentence:

Please open the window. Certainly.

2. after an abbreviation:

The Romans landed in 43 B.C.

(However, 'TV' is now seldom written with full stops.)

3. in many common contractions written as abbreviations:

secy.   mfg.   Ltd.   Inc.   recd.

4. as a decimal point in writing currency figures:

£3·50

and in measurements:

.35 cal.

Exceptions

However, there are exceptions. Here is a brief guide, but for details refer to a good dictionary, e.g. the *Collins English Dictionary*.

1. Abbreviations of compound names of international organizations and national agencies are usually now written without full stops and without spaces:

UN   TUC   BBC   ITA   FT

2. No full stops are used after symbols of chemical elements:

H   Ag   Au   U 235   K

3. No full stops are generally used in lists:

Punctuation
Hints on spelling
A short history of English

4. The terms '1st', '2nd', '3rd', etc., are not abbreviations and need no full stops.

5. Isolated letters of the alphabet used as designations take no full stops:

T square   A4 paper   I beam

6. It is generally customary to omit the full stops from

Mr   Mrs   Ms   Miss   Dr   St
The most important thing here is to be consistent.

**Ellipsis . . .
and quotation**

Ellipsis is a type of punctuation consisting of a row of three full stops or dots (. . .). If the ellipsis comes at the end of a sentence, add an extra full stop as the terminal punctuation, unless a question mark or an exclamation mark is called for.

As ellipsis marks, these full stops indicate the intentional omission from a quotation of one word, several words, a sentence or several sentences. By convention, the terminal full stop is placed *inside* the inverted commas (' ') of the quotation if it is part of a complete sentence, but outside the final inverted commas if the quotation is only a word or a phrase:

As John wrote, 'The rock group was brilliant, but . . . the crowd was . . . unruly . . . .'

Original quotation:

'The rock group was brilliant, but I'm sorry to say that the crowd was very noisy and unruly during most of the concert.'

The comma ,

This causes more problems than all other marks of punctuation. It is the mark used with the widest divergence. Basically, the comma indicates a short pause and then the continuation of the thought of a sentence. Use the comma to set off:

1. main clauses joined by conjunctions, e.g., 'and', 'or', 'nor', 'but', 'so', 'for':

He studied his exam questions thoroughly, for he had to pass this time.

There were few new releases in the record shop, so she went elsewhere to buy the album.

2. sentence elements out of their normal position, e.g., subsidiary clauses before main clauses:

Although the flight was scheduled to depart in the morning, it didn't leave until late afternoon.

When the goal was scored, the crowd went wild.

3. changes of sentence structure found in *informal* writing style:

This is the right room, isn't it?

I thought I'd never get home, the weather was so bad.

4. introductory phrases when they are long or contain verb forms:

On the recommendation of the head of her department and her tutors, the student was allowed to resit her final exams.

5. adjectives immediately following the word they modify:

His hat, large and flamboyant, provoked much comment.

6. certain parenthetical expressions, including such conjunctive adverbs as 'however', 'moreover', 'therefore', etc.:

Her greatest success, however, was in maths.

His strange behaviour, it always seemed to me, was the result of drug addiction.

By the way, the floppy disc is on the table.

7. phrases standing apart from usual sentence construction:

The political situation having been normalized, the troops pulled out.

8. commas are used to set off a non-restrictive clause or phrase following a main clause. Non-restrictive in this sense means that it can be left out *without* altering the meaning of the main clause:

The bombs, which are placed in a special foam solution, are easily detonated.

Compare this sentence:

The bombs that are placed in a special foam solution are easily detonated.

Here, 'that are placed in a special foam solution', identifies the type of bomb and is therefore restrictive. No commas should be used. (Note that 'that' is preferable to 'which' in restrictive clauses.)

9. to separate out direct speech from the speaker:

'I'm not sure about that', said John.

10. words, phrases and clauses of similar construction that occur in a series:

The will mentioned Jane, Paul, and Louis.

The comma before 'and' here is optional, and often not used.

The band was playing, the fans were fainting, the kids were bopping.

11. parts of dates, addresses, etc.:

Wednesday, 4 July 1984, is Independence Day.

She lives at 123 High Street, Chester, Cheshire.

12. before and after 'etc.', 'or the like', 'and so on', when ending a series but not a sentence:

Any man who sings, dances, stars in films, etc., is bound to be useful to advertisers.

13. after 'namely', 'for example', 'that is', 'e.g.', 'i.e.', 'such as', 'as', etc.:

Study-skills training works, e.g., all the students took better notes as a result.

14. between academic or other initials in a series:

Sherlock Watson, B.A., M.A., Ph.D.

15. after the salutation and superscription in a personal letter:

Dear Fred,

16. to set off adjacent sets of figures and (usually) identical words:

In the year 1985, 430 students graduated.

Whatever is, is right.

17. between thousands, millions and other groups of three digits:

1,536   1,350,000

except when naming years of less than five digits:

1100 A.D.   15,000 B.C.

18. to separate off several adjectives preceding a noun but not before the noun itself:

It was a dull, dark, awesome place.

However, if the final adjective identifies the noun, then there should be no commas after it:

It was a large stone pillar (i.e., not a brick one).

Don't overuse the comma

The comma may cause problems, owing to the great variety of its uses. Don't overuse the comma. By doing so you may only confuse the reader. If your sentence is ambiguous, rewrite it. Don't try to sort out a badly constructed sentence by peppering it with commas (or any other

kind of punctuation) in the hope of correcting it. The current convention for the comma is to use it lightly in an open system of punctuation, without creating ambiguity.

The comma splice

Undoubtedly, the worst fault in the use of the comma is the so-called 'comma splice'. Here the comma has been wrongly used in place of a full stop:

> He opened up the engine and roared off, this made the accident unavoidable.

The only cure for this fault is to go back over your writing, read the sentences aloud to yourself and select the more appropriate punctuation.

The semicolon **;**

This is not the easiest punctuation mark to use correctly. It indicates a close relationship between the sentence structures it separates. It balances elements equal in grammatical importance. Implying a longer pause than a comma, but not so long as a full stop, the semicolon helps keep the unity of thought in a long sentence by briefly resting the reader's attention. It should be used:

1. where you wish to break a sentence into two more-or-less equal parts, but because each part is clearly connected you do not wish to use a full stop:

> Many explorers went across the Antarctic Plateau; many more went to their deaths amongst the great crevasses.

2. to separate independent clauses of a compound sentence where there is no connective word or phrase:

> Do not surrender; resist to the last.

or, where there is a pointed contrast between the clauses:

> A fool talks incessantly; a wise man holds his tongue.

3. between clauses connected by conjunctive adverbs, such as: 'accordingly', 'also', 'consequently', furthermore', 'hence', 'however', 'nevertheless', 'otherwise', 'so', 'therefore', 'thus', etc.:

> You recommended this student; therefore, I will consider him for the job.

4. where the clauses contain commas, and the clauses are separated by 'and' or 'but':

> The seasons come and go, and the years pass on; but taxes never end.

5. to separate the items in a series of clauses or phrases introduced by a colon especially if the clauses or phrases are long and/or contain commas:

> The percentages increased yearly: 1980, 25%; 1981, 32%; 1983, 39%; 1984, 41%.

6. in lists of names with addresses, titles, or figures, where a comma alone would not separate items or references clearly:

The rock star has homes in Beverly Hills, California; Cannes, France; and London, England.

Deut. 3:1-10; 4:4-6.

Placing semicolons

The convention is to place semicolons outside inverted commas and curved brackets:

The vote was almost unanimous in favour of the motion (three members abstained); but, in the end, the action taken did not succeed. They heard much cheering and cries of 'Hear! Hear!'; but to no result.

The colon :

This is a strong separator, and is often used in an introductory way. It tells the reader that the part of the sentence following the colon adds to, elaborates on, or explains the preceding statement. It should be used:

1. to introduce a direct quotation:

As Stalin said: 'And how many battalions has the Pope?'

2. a list:

These are his favourites: John Lennon, David Bowie and Marvin Gaye.

3. an explanatory clause:

This was her clever argument: if she had not taken the cash, her brother would have spent it.

4. to separate the parts of numerical ratios:

12:25 x:57

5. between Biblical chapter and verse numbers, between volume and page numbers, in references using Arabic numerals; and between places of publication and publisher's name in bibliographical references and footnotes:

1 Corinthians 13:4-7.

Journal of Computing 12:152 (1983).

Burns, C. *Computers*. London: Science Press, 1982.

6. between corresponding words placed in pairs for comparison:

The stature of the two sexes shows almost the same male:female proportions.

7. between the main part of the title and the sub-title:

The Lion Rises: A History of Scotland.

The question mark ?

This is used at the end of a direct statement writtten as a question:

When will you learn to use the question mark correctly?

When not to use it

Don't use the question mark:

1. for an indirect question:

She didn't know why she omitted the question mark.

2. after certain kinds of polite request, use a full stop instead:

Will you please fill in this form.

Uses

A question mark, enclosed in curved brackets, is used after a word, phrase or date to indicate uncertainty about its accuracy or a gap in available information:

Omar Khayyám, Persian poet (?-1123?)

Question marks may occasionally be used within a sentence in a series of short phrases or clauses:

When they reached Paris, where did they go for food? — for lodgings? — for work?

Note that the question mark is placed *inside* inverted commas only if the quoted words are interrogative:

She asked, 'What is a question mark?'

The exclamation mark ! This is used after an interjection (such as 'ah', 'wow', 'whew', 'alas', etc.) and after any phrase or sentence expressing wish, command or irony, to indicate forceful emphasis or strong feeling:

I wish I had won that million pound game!

Don't overuse the exclamation mark as an easy means of emphasizing an idea. The structure of the sentence itself should convey the emphasis.

The dash — This is used to indicate a sudden break in thought and in the structure of the sentence:

A throbbing, repetitive beat at 120 decibels — that's disco music for a bored generation.

Use a pair of dashes to set off parenthetical expressions that require punctuation more distinct than commas:

Her great success — three gold records, parts in West End musicals — seemed worthless to her during her near-fatal illness.

In such contexts as this, dashes and curved brackets can be used interchangeably.

Other uses

A dash is used between extreme dates or numbers, and often in joining capitalized two-word names:

pages 16—67

the decade 1971—81

London—Paris flight

**Curved brackets ** These, also called parentheses, are used to set off a word, a phrase or a clause which is inserted in a sentence by way of comment or explanation.

Don't put the opening curve at the end of a line, or the closing curve at the beginning of one.

Don't clutter up the sentence with curved brackets. Use them sensibly.

Curved brackets may create a special effect — humorous or pathetic or ironic — in a sentence:

If you want my opinion (but nobody does), he should have stayed in Liverpool.

Curved brackets can be used to enclose numbers or letters within a sentence:

There are three steps in the procedure: (1) open the packet; (2) empty the contents into a mug; and (3) add boiling water.

The closing curved bracket is sometimes used by itself when a list is arranged vertically:

These are the main expenses in running the society:
a) postage
b) telephone charges
c) stationery

Curved brackets may also be used to enclose the English translation of foreign words and phrases:

Noli me tangere (Touch me not)

When curved brackets are used, with the concluding bracket occurring at the end of the sentence, the full stop is placed *outside* the concluding curve:

The tape should be a C90 cassette (or C120 if there is much to record).

If, however, the enclosed expression is a separate complete sentence, the full stop goes *within* the end bracket:

(By the way, I saw your friend Alice the other day.)

Square brackets   []   These are used to set off words or figures inserted in a text. Use them to enclose:

1. any editorial insertion in a quotation:

'When he [Mr Churchill] spoke at the meeting.'
'That winter [1943] was the worst of the war.'

2. parentheses within parentheses or curved brackets:

The programme was devoted to jazz (lots of Armstrong songs [two of them rarely heard] and King Oliver numbers).

However, such constructions are clumsy and difficult to read. Avoid them if possible.

The hyphen   -   This is used to join words to express a single idea, especially when a group of words is being used as an adjective (e.g., 'a once-in-a-lifetime trip) and to divide words into syllables (e.g., 'hy-phen'), particularly when splitting between two lines of text.

Different opinions   Authorities differ in their opinion about which compounds are to be written as single words, as two words, or as hyphenated words. The following guide represents the generally accepted current usage, but whenever there is any doubt or question, consult a good, up-to-date dictionary.

Compounds are usually written as single words when the first element is a prefix (<u>un</u>conscious) or a combining form (<u>tele</u>vision), or when the last element is a suffix (quick<u>ly</u>), or a combining form (bio<u>logy</u>).

Common combinations of words that are unhyphenated when they function as nouns, e.g.:

dead end   nineteenth century   peaches and cream

are hyphenated when they are used as adjectives preceding the noun they qualify:

dead-end road   nineteenth-century china

peaches-and-cream complexion

The use of hyphens here helps to avoid ambiguity.

Hyphenation is not necessary when proper nouns consisting of two or more words are used adjectively, as the use of capitals ensures clarity:

Third World countries   Cold War atmosphere

United Nations initiatives

Some uses

Compounds are hyphenated when:

1. the second element is capitalized or represents an official institution or person:

Anglo-American   ex-premier

2. words are put together in temporary or repetitive combinations:

caught-red-handed   trudge-trudge-trudge

3. the word combination contains a prepositional phrase:

up-to-date   sister-in-law

4. the first element is 'self':

self-satisfaction   self-reliant

5. a compound word must be distinguished from a word of different meaning that would otherwise have the same spelling:

re-creation   not   recreation

re-form   not   reform

re-cover   not   recover

6. where the same letter occurs three times in succession and would annoy the reader:

bell-like   skill-less   cross-stitch

7. where a vowel would be confusingly doubled in combination — equally annoying to the reader:

anti-imperialist   co-owner   pre-empt   re-enter

But note that the words 'cooperative' and 'coordinate' are usually written as single words, although they can also be written as hyphenated words: 'co-operation', 'co-ordinate'.

8. where it is necessary to avoid an ambiguous combination of vowels:

cave-in   drive-in   flare-up   mop-up

9. use the hyphen to join words in compound numbers from twenty-one to ninety-nine.

Other uses

Use the hyphen to divide words into syllables at the end of a line where you cannot fit in the whole word. You can hyphenate between any of the syllables of a word, although ideally it is best to have more than two letters in either half. You can find out how the word divides into syllables by saying it aloud to yourself slowly. If two consonants are found together and do not obviously belong to the one syllable, place the hyphen in between them, e.g.:

im-mense   pret-tily   har-bour   sum-mation

Do not break words that are already hyphenated except at the hyphen, e.g.:

An-glo-American

is not permitted. If in doubt then consult a large dictionary such as *Collins English Dictionary* which shows where every word can be hyphenated.

The apostrophe ,

This is used to denote the omission of one or more letters in the spelling of a word, and to indicate possession for singular and plural nouns and the indefinite pronoun 'one'. Here are its uses:

Uses

1. the absence of letters in a word is seen in contractions with the apostrophe, e.g.:

can't   don't   won't   you're

A common mistake is the confusion between 'its' and 'it's': 'it's' is the contraction of 'it is', while 'its' is the neuter possessive:

It's [it is] raining

Its [the album's] cover is well designed

There is also confusion over 'your' and 'you're'.

You're [you are] not staying out late.

Your record is broken.

2. the absence of letters in a word is also seen in written equivalents of dialect, as in these lines from 'The Jolly Beggars' by Robert Burns:

I am a bard of no regard,
    Wi' gentle folks, and a' that:
But, Homer-like, the glowrin' byke,
    Frae town to town I draw that.

3. to indicate missing digits in a date:

hit records of '84

Forming possessives

The other main use of the apostrophe is in creating possessive forms of singular and plural nouns and the indefinite pronoun 'one', with the letter 's'.

The apostrophe comes before the 's' in the singular form:

> a woman's rights   one's self control

The apostrophe follows the 's' in possessive plurals:

> the boys' jeans   some families' resources

Add ''s' to form possessive plurals when the plural does not end in 's':

> children's tricks   women's votes

To form the possessive singular of words ending in 's' add ''s', not just the apostrophe alone:

> Robert Burns's poems   Dickens's novels

But the convention is that it should be:

> Jesus' [*not* Jesus's] teachings

However, some authorities allow both the -*s'* and the -*s's* forms. Again be consistent with the style you adopt.

Uses with or without the 's'

Other conventional uses of the apostrophe, with or without the 's', involve:

1. certain words preceding the word 'sake':

> for goodness' sake   for convenience' sake

but note:

> for appearance's sake   for science's sake

2. adding 's' to make the possessive of titles, firm names, initials, abbreviations, etc.:

> Elizabeth II's reign   the BBC's programmes

3. forming the possessive of words of time duration:

> a week's holiday   ten minutes' wait

4. an apostrophe followed by an 's' may be used to form the plurals of figures, letters and signs of words:

> He got 3A's, 2B's and 3C's in his finals.

but note that 'the 1930s' is generally preferred to 'the 1930's' — although consistency is the main thing.

Inverted commas (quotation marks)
' ' " "

Both " " and ' ' are used to set off a direct quotation, that is the direct words taken from another source, such as a writer or speaker:

> The reviewer of the new book on The Rolling Stones said, 'It is the best, most interesting study of this group yet published.'
> Another reviewer of the same book criticized it for 'some sloppy writing and factual errors', but thought that it would sell well.

Notice that in the first example, the full stop goes inside the final inverted commas because the quotation is a complete sentence. In the second example, the comma goes outside the final inverted commas because the quoted words are only a fragment of a sentence, and the comma is not part of the quotation itself, but part of the punctuation of the whole sentence containing the quotation.

By convention, the semicolon and colon always go outside inverted commas, while the question mark and the exclamation mark go inside or outside according to the sense of the sentence.

Alternative to inverted commas

An alternative to using inverted commas in quoting long passages (say three or more lines) is to set the quotation apart from the rest of the text, with a 1 cm indentation, wider margins and single spacing if the material is typed:

> The reviewer of the new book on The Rolling Stones said:
>
> > It is the best, most interesting study of this group ever published. Not only does it give us a vivid picture of the individual characters, but it also analyses their musical development with insight and intelligence. I highly recommend it.

Quoting verse

The same may be done with more than a line or two of poetry or song lyric, but always keep the poet's line length. See the quotation from Robert Burns in the apostrophe section as an example.

If you quote a short section of poetry within inverted commas in your main text, indicate the poet's line division with oblique strokes:

> In the passage 'To die, to sleep; / To sleep, perchance to dream', Shakespeare sums up the uncertainty of death.

Paragraphing and inverted commas

When you are quoting two or more paragraphs using inverted commas, place these marks at the beginning of each paragraph, but at the end of only the final paragraph:

> 'Paragraph 1 of quoted text— .
>
> 'Paragraph 2 of quoted text — .'

Dialogue

Use inverted commas to indicate speech in a dialogue, with the speakers' names or equivalent pronouns and verbs outside the inverted commas:

> 'I really fancy that new boy in the class,' she admitted, 'but I'm afraid I wouldn't have a chance with him.'

Inverted commas may also be used for implied speech:

> Her glance seemed to say, 'Just dare me to do it.'

Double inverted commas

Double inverted commas are usually used for quotations within quotations:

> The general reminisced: 'I well remember the day that Churchill delivered his famous "their finest hour" speech.'

Titles

Use inverted commas to enclose the titles of short poems, stories, essays, articles in magazines and newspapers, chapters of books, single records, songs, etc. The conventional usage is to italicize (if you are writing or using a typewriter, underline) the titles of longer works, such as textbooks, novels, plays, LP albums and the like:

> the article 'Video Discs' published in the *New Musical Express*
>
> Tolstoy's short story 'The Kreutzer Sonata' and his novel *War and Peace.*
>
> the song 'When I'm Sixty-Four' on the *Sgt. Pepper* album

Other uses

Use inverted commas to enclose words when those words themselves are under discussion:

> The terms 'feedback' and 'byte' are computer jargon.

Capitals

Capital letters are used at the beginnings of all proper nouns, that is, nouns that distinguish some individual person, place or thing from others in the same class, and also at the beginnings of all adjectives that derive their descriptive meaning from the person, place or thing named by the noun.

Uses

Capitalize the initial letters of a person's name, and the title of a person when it comes before the person's name:

> King Kong
>
> The Right Honourable Herbert Grump

However when you are writing about 'the kings and queens of Great Britain' or 'British prime ministers', use initial lower case letters for the words 'kings', 'queens' and 'prime ministers'.

Capitalize the major words in the titles of books, plays, films, LP albums and the like:

> *Lord of the Rings*

where the major words are *'Lord'* and *'Rings'*, but if *'of'* (or some other preposition) or the articles *'the'*, *'an'* or *'a'* form the first word of the title, they too, should be capitalized:

> *Of Human Bondage*
>
> *The Grapes of Wrath*

With newspapers and magazines, however, the initial article, 'the', is neither capitalized nor italicised (or underlined):

> the *Evening Times*

unless the word 'the' is a proper part of the complete title:

> *The Times*

'I'

Capitalize the first word in any sentence, and the first person singular, nominative case, 'I', is always capitalized in English, no matter where it comes in the sentence.

When using hyphenated compounds, capitalize only the first word of the compound:

> Forty-ninth Street

except when nouns are used in title:

> The Man—Woman Conflict

Capitalize points of the compass only when they designate specific areas of a country or of the world:

> The sun rises in the east.
>
> The South was in conflict with the North in the American Civil War.

Don't capitalize names of subjects studied unless they are exact titles of specific courses or are already proper names:

> He was a student in the Department of Civil Engineering at Cathcart Polytechnic.
>
> She didn't like physics.
>
> She failed her exam in Physics II.

Italics

The type of print called *italics* is represented in handwriting or typing by underlining. It is used chiefly to distinguish words for importance and emphasis. We have already touched on this aspect in the section on quotation.

Italicize Latin scientific names of genera, species, subspecies and varieties in botanical and zoological names:

> The great white heron *(Ardea occidentalis)* is found in Florida and Mexico.

Italicize foreign words that have not been naturalized into English:

> *noblesse*   *Zeitgeist*   *Anschluss*

Many words have now been naturalized, so again, if in doubt, consult a good dictionary.

SUMMARY OF THE MAIN POINTS

■ Effective punctuation is there to help the reader make sense of what you have written. It is a guide to the sense that you intended.

■ Good punctuation, no matter how well done, can never compensate for loose sentence construction or careless grammar leading to ambiguity.

■ The best way to learn punctuation is to study closely how good writers use it. Become critical as you read texts.

■ Always, before submitting a final draft, read it and double check that you have enough punctuation to make your sense completely clear.

Further Reading

Carey, G.V.   *Mind the Stop.* Penguin, 1976.

Evans, H.   *Editing and Design, Book 1:*
                   Newsman's English.
                   Heinemann, 1972.

Hanks, P.,   *Collins English Dictionary.*
editor.   Collins, 1979.

Turabian, K.L.   *A Manual for Writers.*
                   Heinemann, 1982.

Chapter 7   Spelling and Use of the Dictionary

Spelling matters

Many students seem to give little thought to spelling, as if it doesn't matter much. But spelling does matter, especially to prospective employers and examiners who have occasion to read and assess students' writing, which may be seriously marred by errors in spelling.

Misspellings create a bad impression

In a letter of application for a job, misspellings create an impression of illiteracy or inadequate education, as in this example:

> Dear Perso<u>na</u>l Officer,
>   I have rec<u>ie</u>ved your letter . . . .

In an essay or a report, misspellings betray the student's ignorance or carelessness or possibly both, and may adversely affect the grade given to the work. Dictionaries are readily available, so there is no excuse for misspellings to remain in final drafts of your letters, essays, reports and other texts.

Rules and exceptions to be learned

The spelling of many English words does present problems. There are, of course, rules for spelling, which should be learned because they have wide application. There are, too, many exceptions to the rules, which must also be learned.

Prefixes

First we will consider some of the most common prefixes and suffixes (of Latin or Greek origin) which are used in English.

When the prefixes 'e-' and 'in-' are followed by 'r', 'l', or 'm', the 'in-' becomes 'ir-', 'il-' or 'im-', thus doubling the consonant, while 'e-' stays unchanged in all combinations. The following words with these prefixes are those most commonly misspelled:

55

emigrate	illegible
eminent	irrelevant
elude	illicit
erect	immigrate
elicit	imminent

Before 'b' or 'p', 'in-' becomes 'im-', as in 'imbue' and 'impudent', but before 'd' and 's', 'in-' does not change, for example, in 'indict' and 'insidious'.

With such other prefixes as 'ad-', 'con-', 'dis-', and 'sub-', in which the consonant changes, the following letter is doubled, for example:

accessory
alleviate
aggravate
correct
diffident
resurrection

An exception here is 'ameliorate'.

Suffixes

Students are often uncertain when to use such pairs of suffixes as '-able'/'-ible', '-ative'/'-itive', '-acious'/'-icious'. Unless the students have a knowledge of Latin, they will have to learn the individual words. The most frequently misspelled words with these suffixes are:

irritable	exhaustible
indispensable	responsible
comparative	definitive
avaricious	voracious

Use of the suffixes '-ent' and '-ant' also causes confusion. Again, students must learn how each word is spelled. The most frequently misspelled words of this type are:

adherent	cogent
contingent	dependent (adjective)
imminent	dependant (noun)
conversant	impudent
relevant	dominant
insolent	resonant
flagrant	

Doubling final consonants

When a word ends in a single consonant preceded by a single vowel and is accented on the final syllable, double the final consonant when adding a syllable. For example:

begin	beginning
refer	referred
occur	occurred

An exception is 'appeal, appealing'.

When similar words are not accented on the final syllable, the final consonant is not doubled. For example:

develop	developed
benefit	benefited

An exception is 'worship, worshipped'.

Such words as 'all', 'full', 'fill', 'well', and 'till' lose the second 'l' when they are combined as first or last syllables in compound words. For example:

almighty	awful	fulfil
until	spoonful	handful
welcome		

Exceptions are: 'farewell', 'wellborn', 'illness', and 'smallness'. Note, however, that 'all right' is *two* words, *not* the single word 'alright'.

In addition, here are some words commonly misspelled with double consonants where they should be single, or with single consonants where they should be double:

adopt	adept
disappear	disappoint
disaster	discriminate
relative	parallel
occasionally	

These are words often incorrectly spelled with the double consonants written as single ones:

accessory	accommodate
apposite	attempt
vaccinate	vacillate

There are many other instances where general rules can help you. But since there are often as many exceptions as examples, we will mention only the most frequently used, rather than attempt to present a comprehensive coverage, which would prolong this chapter excessively. When you have any question about spelling, consult your dictionary.

Helpful spelling rules

These are some helpful spelling rules to know:

1. Nouns and verbs derived from the same root sometimes cause confusion. The noun ends in 'ce-', the verb in '-se'. For example:

nouns	*verbs*
device	devise
practice	practise
licence	license

2. Abstract nouns formed from adjectives ending in '-ate', or from other nouns ending in '-at', take '-acy' endings. For example:

adjectives	*nouns*
accurate	accuracy
private	privacy

nouns	*abstract nouns*
autocrat	autocracy
democrat	democracy

3. Nouns ending in '-y' form their plurals by adding '-ies', except where the '-y' is preceded by a vowel. For example:

nanny	nannies
lady	ladies
body	bodies
penny	pennies

but

chimney	chimneys
valley	valleys
journey	journeys

The word 'money' has two plurals, with slightly different meanings: 'moneys' and 'monies', the latter in the sense of sums of money.

4. Verbs ending in '-y' preceded by a consonant form the past tense or past participle by changing the '-y' to '-ied'. For example:

embody	embodied
rally	rallied
apply	applied
rely	relied

Note that the '-y' is kept when the ending itself begins with an 'i', as in

apply	applying
reply	replying

This avoids an awkward double 'i'.

5. For words ending in an unsounded '-e', drop the 'e' when adding a suffix beginning with a vowel. For example:

debate	debatable
value	valuable
care	caring
excite	excitable

But note: 'change' and 'changeable'. However, the '-e' is retained before a suffix beginning with a consonant, for example:

excite	excitement
value	valueless
care	carefree

7. When a syllable rhymes with 'see', the 'i' comes before 'e' except after 'c'. For example:

piece	believe	retrieve	achieve
receive	receipt	deceive	

There are a few other notable exceptions, such as:

| weird | seize | weir | counterfeit |

8. Take care spelling words to which the suffixes '-sion' and '-tion' are added. For example:

possess	possession
appreciate	appreciation

All verbs ending with '-de' take '-sion', such as:

provide	provision
deride	derision

9. Note the spellings of endings using '-city' and '-sity', as in

publi<u>c</u>	publi<u>c</u>ity
perver<u>se</u>	perver<u>s</u>ity

10. The '-cede' and '-ceed' endings sometimes cause trouble. You must learn which are the correct spellings. For example:

proceed (but proc<u>e</u>dure)	precede
succeed	concede
exceed	accede

11. In the use of '-ise' and '-ize' there is some debate among experts. We have favoured '-ize' (as in 'specialize') in this book, following the preference of the *Collins English Dictionary* and the norms used in *The Times* and the *Encyclopedia Britannica*. There is no choice, however, where '-ise' is not a suffix but part of the main word. For example:

supervise	revise	advise
surprise	arise	devise
advertise	analyse	

Words sounding the same, with different spellings, meanings

Take great care with words which have the same or nearly the same pronunciation, but differ in their spellings and meanings. For example:

affect	(verb):	Wars affect people.
effect	(noun):	The effect of wars.
canvas	(noun):	The tent is made of canvas.
canvass	(verb):	Please canvass your group.
compliment	(noun):	She paid him a compliment on his performance.
complement	(noun):	The complement of the yacht is six.
council	(noun):	The town council met today.
counsel	(verb):	I counsel you to accept the job.
	(noun):	I asked my counsel for advice.
current	(noun):	The electrical current failed.
currant	(noun):	This cake is full of black currants.
dependant	(noun):	Your father is your dependant.
dependent	(adjective):	His future is dependent on the examinations.
devise	(verb):	Did you devise the scheme?
device	(noun):	It's a cunning device for a bomb.
elicit	(verb):	Can you elicit a response from him?
illicit	(adjective):	The whisky was illicit.
emigrate	(verb):	He emigrated from India.
immigrate	(verb):	He immigrated into Britain.
eminent	(adjective):	Churchill was an eminent statesman.
imminent	(adjective):	Nuclear war is imminent.
immanent	(meaning 'inherent'; adjective):	God is immanent in nature.
exhausting	(adjective):	The marathon was exhausting.
exhaustive	(adjective):	His investigation was exhaustive.

| ensure | (verb): | Locks ensure safety. |
| insure | (verb): | You must insure your jewels against theft. |

| flare | (noun): | He saw a flare of light in the wood. |
| flair | (noun): | He has a flair for art. |

its (possessive pronoun): The book had lost its cover.
it's (contraction of 'it is'): It's on the table.

| key | (noun): | Give me the key to the room. |
| quay | (noun): | The boats moored up by the quay. |

| lightning | (noun): | She saw a flash of lightning before the thunder crashed. |
| lightening | (verb): | Lightening his load, he moved faster. |

| passed | (verb): | He passed her on the street. |
| past | (adjective): | Most past ages were violent. |

| personal | (adjective): | It was a personal letter. |
| personnel | (noun): | The office personnel had a Christmas party. |

| principle | (noun): | The principle of flight. |
| principal | (adjective): | The principal author of the day. |

| practice | (noun): | The practice of medicine. |
| practise | (verb): | He wanted to practise medicine. |

| recourse | (noun): | His only recourse was to quit. |
| resource | (noun): | Coal is an important natural resource. |

| septic | (adjective): | His wound was septic. |
| sceptic | (adjective): | He was a sceptic in religion. |

| stationary | (adjective): | The train was stationary on the tracks. |
| stationery | (noun): | Note paper and envelopes are in the stationery department. |

their (possessive pronoun): Their book is on the table.
| there | (adverb): | The book is there on the table. |
they're (contraction of 'they are'): They're my books.

too	(adverb):	The film was too long.
		She, too, had the 'flu.
to	(preposition):	He went to the door and opened it.
two	(adjective):	There were two books on the table.

| waste | (adjective): | The waste land was very grim. |
| waist | (noun): | She has a very slim waist. |

| your | (pronoun): | It is your turn now. |
you're (contraction of 'you are'): You're the only one to succeed.

I DON'T BELIEVE IT!

A sceptic tank

Plurals of certain foreign words

Certain foreign words adopted into English still form their plurals in the manner of the original language (usually Latin). For example:

appendix, appendices (also appendixes)
addendum, addenda
criterion, criteria
formula, formulae (also formulas)

SAMPLE PAGE OF DICTIONARY

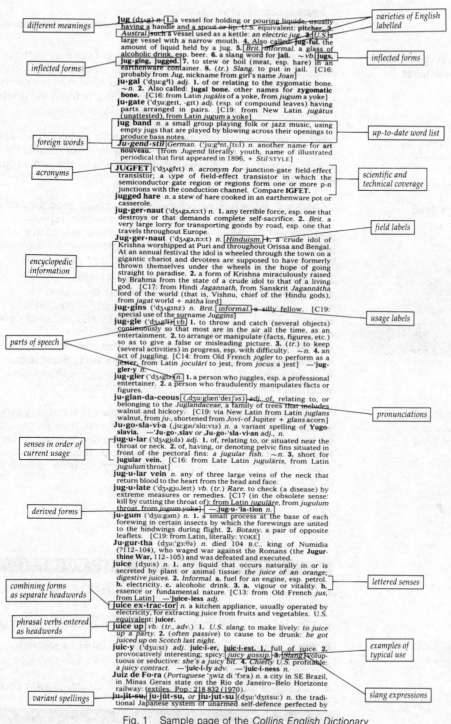

different meanings

jug (dʒʌɡ) *n.* **1.** a vessel for holding or pouring liquids, usually having a handle and a spout or lip. U.S. equivalent: **pitcher. 2.** *Austral.* such a vessel used as a kettle: *an electric jug.* **3.** *U.S.* a large vessel with a narrow mouth. **4.** Also called: **jug·ful.** the amount of liquid held by a jug. **5.** *Brit. informal.* a glass of alcoholic drink, esp. beer. **6.** a slang word for **jail.** ~*vb.* **jugs, jug·ging, jugged. 7.** to stew or boil (meat, esp. hare) in an earthenware container. **8.** (*tr.*) *Slang.* to put in jail. [C16: probably from *Jug,* nickname from girl's name *Joan*]

varieties of English labelled

inflected forms

inflected forms

ju·gal ('dʒuːɡ²l) *adj.* **1.** of or relating to the zygomatic bone. ~*n.* **2.** Also called: **jugal bone.** other names for **zygomatic bone.** [C16: from Latin *jugális* of a yoke, from *jugum* a yoke]

ju·gate ('dʒuːɡeɪt, -ɡɪt) *adj.* (esp. of compound leaves) having parts arranged in pairs. [C19: from New Latin *jugátus* (unattested), from Latin *jugum* a yoke]

jug band *n.* a small group playing folk or jazz music, using empty jugs that are played by blowing across their openings to produce bass notes.

up-to-date word list

foreign words

Ju·gend·stil *German.* ('juːɡ²nt͵ʃtiːl) *n.* another name for **art nouveau.** [from *Jugend* literally: youth, name of illustrated periodical that first appeared in 1896, + *Stil* STYLE]

acronyms

JUGFET ('dʒʌɡfɛt) *n.* *acronym for* junction-gate field-effect transistor; a type of field-effect transistor in which the semiconductor gate region or regions form one or more p-n junctions with the conduction channel. Compare **IGFET.**

scientific and technical coverage

jugged hare *n.* a stew of hare cooked in an earthenware pot or casserole.

jug·ger·naut ('dʒʌɡə͵nɔːt) *n.* **1.** any terrible force, esp. one that destroys or that demands complete self-sacrifice. **2.** *Brit.* a very large lorry for transporting goods by road, esp. one that travels throughout Europe.

field labels

Jug·ger·naut ('dʒʌɡə͵nɔːt) *n.* *Hinduism.* **1.** a crude idol of Krishna worshipped at Puri and throughout Orissa and Bengal. At an annual festival the idol is wheeled through the town on a gigantic chariot and devotees are supposed to have formerly thrown themselves under the wheels in the hope of going straight to paradise. **2.** a form of Krishna miraculously raised by Brahma from the state of a crude idol to that of a living god. [C17: from Hindi *Jagannath,* from Sanskrit *Jagannātha* lord of the world (that is, Vishnu, chief of the Hindu gods), from *jagat* world + *nātha* lord]

encyclopedic information

jug·gins ('dʒʌɡɪnz) *n.* *Brit. informal.* a silly fellow. [C19: special use of the surname *Juggins*]

jug·gle ('dʒʌɡ²l) *vb.* **1.** to throw and catch (several objects) continuously so that most are in the air all the time, as an entertainment. **2.** to arrange or manipulate (facts, figures, etc.) so as to give a false or misleading picture. **3.** (*tr.*) to keep (several activities) in progress, esp. with difficulty. ~*n.* **4.** an act of juggling. [C14: from Old French *jogler* to perform as a jester, from Latin *joculárī* to jest, from *jocus* a jest] —**'jug·gler·y** *n.*

usage labels

parts of speech

jug·gler ('dʒʌɡlə) *n.* **1.** a person who juggles, esp. a professional entertainer. **2.** a person who fraudulently manipulates facts or figures.

ju·glan·da·ceous (͵dʒuːɡlæn'deɪʃəs) *adj.* of, relating to, or belonging to the *Juglandaceae,* a family of trees that includes walnut and hickory. [C19: via New Latin from Latin *juglans* walnut, from *ju-,* shortened from *Jovi-* of Jupiter + *glans* acorn]

pronunciations

Ju·go·sla·vi·a (͵juːɡəʊ'slɑːvɪə) *n.* a variant spelling of **Yugo-slavia.** —**Ju·go-,slav** *or* ,**Ju·go-'sla·vi·an** *adj., n.*

jug·u·lar ('dʒʌɡjʊlə) *adj.* **1.** of, relating to, or situated near the throat or neck. **2.** of, having, or denoting pelvic fins situated in front of the pectoral fins: *a jugular fish.* ~*n.* **3.** short for **jugular vein.** [C16: from Late Latin *jugulāris,* from Latin *jugulum* throat]

senses in order of current usage

jug·u·lar vein *n.* any of three large veins of the neck that return blood to the heart from the head and face.

jug·u·late ('dʒʌɡjʊ͵leɪt) *vb.* (*tr.*) *Rare.* to check (a disease) by extreme measures or remedies. [C17 (in the obsolete sense: kill by cutting the throat of): from Latin *jugulāre,* from *jugulum* throat, from *jugum* yoke] —**jug·u·'la·tion** *n.*

derived forms

ju·gum ('dʒuːɡəm) *n.* **1.** a small process at the base of each forewing in certain insects by which the forewings are united to the hindwings during flight. **2.** *Botany.* a pair of opposite leaflets. [C19: from Latin, literally: YOKE]

Ju·gur·tha (dʒuː'ɡɜːθə) *n.* died 104 B.C., king of Numidia (?112–104), who waged war against the Romans (the **Jugur-thine War,** 112–105) and was defeated and executed.

juice (dʒuːs) *n.* **1.** any liquid that occurs naturally in or is secreted by plant or animal tissue: *the juice of an orange; digestive juices.* **2.** *Informal.* **a.** fuel for an engine, esp. petrol. **b.** electricity. **c.** alcoholic drink. **3. a.** vigour or vitality. **b.** essence or fundamental nature. [C13: from Old French *jus,* from Latin] —**'juice·less** *adj.*

lettered senses

combining forms as separate headwords

juice ex·trac·tor *n.* a kitchen appliance, usually operated by electricity, for extracting juice from fruits and vegetables. U.S. equivalent: **juicer.**

phrasal verbs entered as headwords

juice up *vb.* (*tr., adv.*) **1.** *U.S. slang.* to make lively: *to juice up a party.* **2.** (*often passive*) to cause to be drunk: *he got juiced up on Scotch last night.*

juic·y ('dʒuːsɪ) *adj.* **juic·i·er, juic·i·est. 1.** full of juice. **2.** provocatively interesting; spicy: *juicy gossip.* **3.** *Slang.* volup-tuous or seductive: *she's a juicy bit.* **4.** *Chiefly U.S.* profitable: *a juicy contract.* —**'juic·i·ly** *adv.* —**'juic·i·ness** *n.*

examples of typical use

Juiz de Fo·ra (*Portuguese* 'ʒwiz dɪ 'fɔrə) *n.* a city in SE Brazil, in Minas Gerais state on the Rio de Janeiro–Belo Horizonte railway; textiles. Pop.: 218 832 (1970).

slang expressions

variant spellings

ju·jit·su, ju·jut·su, *or* **jiu·jut·su** (dʒuː'dʒɪtsuː) *n.* the tradi-tional Japanese system of unarmed self-defence perfected by

Fig. 1   Sample page of the *Collins English Dictionary*

index, indices (also indexes)
medium, media (but mediums for plural of spiritualist medium)
phenomenon, phenomena

Almost everyone makes spelling mistakes

Almost everyone makes mistakes in spelling. They may be the result of carelessness or ignorance or both, but it is also true that English spelling is complex and difficult, and poses many problems even to experts. With so many rules and so many exceptions to them to learn and master, it is no wonder that users of English make mistakes in spelling.

Practise spelling your problem words

It is, of course, important to avoid making spelling errors. If you regularly misspell certain words, make a list of them. Practise spelling the words aloud, and write them down again and again, until the correct spellings are firmly fixed in your memory.

Consult a good dictionary

To help you learn the correct spellings, consult a good dictionary. We recommend the *Collins English Dictionary*, and reproduce on the previous page a sample page from it to give you an idea of the kinds of information about words which it contains. Apart from correct (and variant) spellings, the word entries give you:

- different meanings
- inflected forms
- foreign words
- acronyms
- encyclopaedic information
- parts of speech
- senses in current usage
- derivations
- derived forms
- phrasal verbs
- varieties of English
- up-to-date applications
- scientific and technical coverage
- pronunciations
- accounts of all meanings and senses
- examples of typical usage, including slang expressions
- difficult plurals

A good dictionary is a language reference work

A good language dictionary is a reference work that not only lists words alphabetically and defines them, but also records their forms, spellings, pronunciations, grammatical values, usages, and origins. As such, it is an invaluable aid to all users of the language, including students. You should be in possession of a good dictionary and learn to use it to your own best advantage.

SUMMARY OF THE MAIN POINTS

- Correct spelling does matter, because it creates a favourable impression on the reader.
- Learning use of prefixes and suffixes is helpful in improving spelling.
- Rules of spelling, with their exceptions, must be learned.
- Practise problem words.
- Acquire and use a good dictionary, e.g., *Collins English Dictionary*.

Further Reading

| Little, P. | *Communication in Business,* 3rd ed. Longmans, 1977. |
| Woolcott, L. and W. Unwin | *Communication for Business and Secretarial Students.* Macmillan, 1979. |

Fourteen Do's and Don't's in writing good English:

1. Verbs and subjects has to agree.

2. A pronoun must always agree with their reference.

3. Dont omit apostrophes where they belong.

4. Between you and we, it's necessary to use the right case.

5. Proofread your writting to corect mispelling an erors in grammer punctuation, ect.

6. Don't never use a double negative.

7. Don't put in commas, where they don't belong.

8. It's preferred to not split infinitives.

9. A word about incomplete sentences.

10. Don't write run-on sentences put in proper punctuation.

11. Don't join clauses like I do, but as I say.

12. Correct spelling duz matter.

13. Try not to end a sentence a preposition with.

14. Avoid the comma splice, put in the proper punctuation.

Chapter 8

Research, Retrieval of Information, Use of the Library, Summarizing

RESEARCH AND RETRIEVAL OF INFORMATION

Need to retrieve information

To write an effective coursework essay or research report, you will have to retrieve information from a variety of sources. Seldom will you be able to rely on your lecture notes alone. These will probably have to be expanded and developed with additional information.

Finding an aspect

When you are preparing a research project topic, you must first break it down into manageable aspects or sub-topics. Suppose you are interested in a scientific topic such as nuclear energy. The aspect *nuclear power* suggests itself, but you reject this as being too large. Then you consider *advanced gas-cooled reactors* as a possible aspect, although this, too, is probably too extensive, unless you are assigned to write several thousand words and are given a term in which to conduct the research. Finally, you decide on *design problems in advanced gas-cooled reactors*, an aspect of the overall topic which is restricted enough for a research report with prescribed limitations in wordage and scope. The process of reduction that you followed can be diagrammed as an inverted pyramid:

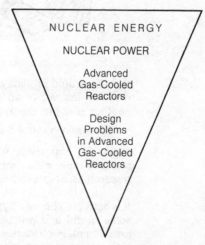

NUCLEAR ENERGY

NUCLEAR POWER

Advanced
Gas-Cooled
Reactors

Design
Problems
in Advanced
Gas-Cooled
Reactors

Fig. 1   Diagram of how to choose a research topic

Setting up a hypothesis

A similar process is followed in selecting an aspect to research in one of the social science areas. You may have to submit a coursework essay developed from investigations carried out during the term. It may, for example, be community-based, as in many social-work courses, or industry-based, as in catering studies. In some subjects, you are required to set up a hypothesis and discuss its validity. You must take care not to select too broad a hypothesis, for example,

> The presence of alcohol in the bloodstream impairs driving ability.

Since there is so much published material on this subject, you would quickly become bogged down in reading the mass of relevant literature,

Restrict the scope of your research.

and you would probably end up writing only a précis of the standard research instead of an original study. Likewise, to investigate, for another example, the hypothesis:

> Television violence contributes towards violence in society

would be impossible without enormous funding, large inputs of research time, wide-ranging research and experiments, and a staff of research assistants to help you.

A useful, practical hypothesis

It is better to choose a hypothesis on which you have a chance of doing some useful and practical investigation, given the restraints of the assignment. For instance, first-year students in further and higher education may receive tuition in study skills, such as note taking and essay writing. Thus, you might set up this hypothesis:

> Induction programmes in study skills help first-year students cope better with the demands placed on them in their courses.

You could devise questionnaires, gather opinions from staff and students, and examine essays, notes, lab reports, etc. You must, of course, guard against drawing unwarranted conclusions from a small-scale survey, but if your results are confirmed by similar investigations done in other institutions, the exercise would be seen to have some value.

Searching for information

Having selected the aspect, or chosen the hypothesis, or been given the coursework essay topic, you will begin the search for information from a variety of sources, such as:

- libraries
- interviews
- questionnaires
- surveys
- experiments and tests
- visits to labs and sites
- personal experience
- video tapes and tape cassettes

- unpublished documents (e.g., letters, diaries, lectures, notes, memos, etc.)
- radio and TV programmes
- pamphlets, brochures, leaflets, etc., obtained from companies
- LP sleeve notes

Dangers of relying on only one source

If you are to be a successful researcher, you must be aware of the many different routes to explore in your search for information. Don't settle for the information found in only one standard textbook or in only one encyclopaedia article. Reliance on just one source of material can result in your essay or report being out of date, biased, too general, or all three of these things, to the detriment of your grade.

System for recording information

You must adopt an efficient system for recording the information you gather. For instance, you might use sheets of A4 paper suitable for filing in a ringbinder notebook, and head each of these with the title of the book, the author's name, and the library classification, or you might use large cards, with information organized like this:

TITLE	AUTHOR	CITY/PUBLISHER	DATE	LIB. REF

Notes

                                                        Page number/numbers

Date notes recorded

Fig. 2   Typical notes page

Such cards can be kept conveniently in a tray or an index box as an easy-to-use reference file.

Record key items of information

Whichever system you adopt, always record the key items of information for each source you use:

1. author's (or authors') name(s)
2. title of book/article/journal

       3. facts of publication:
         a. city of publication
         b. publishers' name
         c. date of publication
         d. edition number where
            applicable

       4. inclusive pages for journal or
          magazine articles

       5. library reference number

In a short-form bibliography, as in our Further Reading lists, the city of publication may be omitted. But in a complete bibliographic entry, as in a technical report, or in an Inter-Library Loan form, it is useful to include the city of publication.

Three bibliographic models

All these items except the library reference numbers will be necessary in writing up the bibliographic entries on your sources to include in your essay or report. Here are three invented models for these entries in standard forms. There are, of course, other standard bibliographic forms, which are equally acceptable. They may vary in punctuation and style, but almost all will contain the same basic information (the city of publication is omitted from some forms for books). If you are in doubt, ask your lecturer for advice. You might also check to see whether your institution has its own 'house style' on bibliographic forms to guide the student. The forms given below can be adapted to your specific needs.

For a book with one author:

     Smith, Fred. *Language and Understanding.*
       New York: Random House, 1970.

For a chapter by two authors in an edited book:

     Brown, Charles and William White. 'The
       Meaning Escapes Me', in *Everyday*
       Communication, George Jones, editor.
       London: Macmillan, 1982.

For a single author of an article in a journal:

     Black, Edward. 'The Art of Communication',
       Cathcart English Review,
       Vol. II, No. 3, Spring 1980, pp. 5-20.

How to enter items in bibliography

These three sources will be entered in your bibliography in alphabetical order by the author's last name:

     Black, Edward . . .

     Brown, Charles and William White . . .
     (the second author here is not being
     listed alphabetically, and so his name
     is written in normal order)

     Smith, Fred . . .

Notice that the second line in each entry is indented half an inch or so (1.25 cm) to give the author's name more prominence to your eye as you look down the bibliography. If you always note down the basic bibliographic information as you conduct your research, you will save yourself a lot of extra time and effort in relocating sources at a later date, in order to copy down the bibliographic facts.

THE LIBRARY

Use of the library

You will probably begin your search for information in the library of your institution. You are responsible for joining the library and for becoming familiar with the layout and services of the library. Study the floorplan, then walk around and explore the premises for yourself. Locate the catalogues, microform readers, reference sections, bound and unbound journals, maps, abstracts and indexes, and the stacks and shelves where books of interest to you are stored.

Get to know your library.

Dewey Decimal System

Most libraries use the Dewey Decimal System of classification by which knowledge is divided into ten headed sections:

000-099	General Works	500-599	Pure Sciences
100-199	Philosophy and Psychology	600-699	Applied Sciences
		700-799	The Arts
200-288	Religion	800-899	Literature
300-399	Social Sciences	900-999	Geography, Biography, History
400-499	Languages		

For example, suppose you want to write a project on some development in the internal combustion engine during the last ten years. Under the DDS classification system, internal combustion engines come at 621.43. This number is determined in the following way:

6 in the first place: Applied Sciences

2 in the second place: Engineering Sciences

1 in the third place: Mechanical and Electrical Engineering

4 after the decimal point: Hot Air Engines

3 last number: Internal Combustion Engines

All the numbers to the left of the decimal point have a higher status than those to the right. 6 is the general classification which narrows down to 621.43.

Here's another example. Suppose you are interested in telecommunications. The books are under 621.38. But on the shelves you will find hundreds of books in many rows, all labelled telecommunications. However, the title of your report is 'Oscillatory Circuit Characteristics', and the DDS classification for that is 621.381533, which is determined as follows:

621 is arrived at as in the previous example

3 first after the decimal point: Electromagnetic Engineering

8 second after the decimal point: Electrical and Communication Engineering

1 third after the decimal point: Electrical Engineering

5 fourth after the decimal point: Short and Longwave Electronics

3 fifth after the decimal point: Circuits

3 sixth after the decimal point: Oscillators

'Secondary interest' of books

Some books may have what is called a 'secondary interest'. For example, a book on colour may be located under physics and the spectrum, but it might also appeal to the artist and the designer of clothes or furniture. It would be impossible to represent all the interests of all possible users of the book.

For a third example, take the subject of communications. Even without considering electronic communications, there are many other DDS Classifications, such as:

Communications: International Relationships: 158.2

Communications: Social Interaction: 302.2

Communications: General: 380.3

Communications: Medical Relationships: 610.696

Communications: Speech-Language Disorders: 616.855

Communications: Personnel Management: 658.3

Communications: Business Methods: 658.45

These are just seven of the classifications for communications under the DDS system. When you consider how much information and knowledge have increased since the Dewey Decimal System was first devised in 1876, when all the classified material was contained in only 24 printed pages, you will understand why the numerous sub-divisions of subject headings have become necessary. A recent edition of the DDS ran to over 3,500 pages.

Library of Congress System

Another widely used system of classification is that devised for the Library of Congress, Washington, D.C., U.S.A. Its 26 divisions are denoted by an initial letter. A second letter indicates a sub-division, and then numbers follow the letters for further refinements. Here is the basic list:

A	Encyclopaedias and Reference Books	M	Music
B	Philosophy, Psychology, Religion	N	Fine Arts
		P	Language and Literature
		Q	Science
C	Antiquities, Biography	R	Medicine
D	History	S	Agriculture and Veterinary Science
E-F	American History		
G	Geography, Anthropology	T	Technology
H	Social Sciences, Economics, Sociology	U	Military Science
		V	Naval Science
I	Political Science	Z	Books and Libraries, Bibliographies
L	Education		

Libraries' common features

No two libraries are exactly alike, but almost all of them have certain features in common. As you become acquainted with the collections and facilities of your own insitutional or municipal library, you will discover what these features are, as well as what is unique about each library. In the U.K. today, most libraries generally contain volumes of books, bound and unbound journals and other periodicals, besides pamphlets, maps, microforms (microfilm and microfiche), audiovisual material and equipment, and photocopying equipment. If you have any problem in locating what you are searching for, don't hesitate to seek help from the library staff — they are always pleased to help.

Arrangement of books

The books are arranged on the shelves in order according to the DDS system. Pamphlets are normally kept in special boxes collected within the main sequence throughout the library.

Catalogues

Two main catalogues—the traditional card catalogue and the computer-produced microfiche catalogue — record the library's stock of books. To ensure a thorough search for information, you must check both catalogues, because the microfiche will probably record only the most recent acquisitions to the library's stock, while the card catalogue records the earlier acquisitions. It is likely that in the major academic and municipal libraries the microfiche catalogue will supersede and eventually replace the card catalogue entirely. The PAC (Public Access Catalogue), which is on-line computer-linked, is likely to supersede both.

Each catalogue has two files

Each catalogue has a number of files. Normally one locates specific items alphabetically by the names of their individual or multiple

If in doubt, ask the library staff.

authors, and perhaps by their titles too. Another file, a classified subject catalogue, shows all the works available on any given subject, and locates specific items where only the subject is known.

Audiovisual

Sound tape cassettes, video tapes, and tape-slide programmes, along with the equipment to use them, may also be available to you in rooms especially allocated for audiovisual studies. Microfilm and microfiche readers are generally kept close to the film files for convenient use.

Periodicals

Journals, magazines and newspapers are kept in the periodical section of the library. Current numbers are out on open display racks to be used as you wish. Unbound back issues are usually available upon application at the periodicals counter. Bound volumes of journals are normally filed within the main library collection. The serials catalogue for periodicals shows the shelf mark for bound volumes and the library's holdings of each title.

The reference collection

The reference collection includes abstracts, indexes and bibliographies (shelf mark 01); encyclopaedias, handbooks, and general reference works (shelf mark 03); language and subject dictionaries (shelf mark 030.8); directories and yearbooks (shelf mark 058); atlases and maps (in the map room or area); and academic calendars and prospectuses.

The permanent reserve collection

The permanent reserve collection consists of textbooks and other documents in large and constant demand for academic courses. Books which are recommended reading for courses or specific projects are usually kept in the temporary reserve collection. The books are catalogued by author and title in a strip index, while a rotary index lists in two sequences (by authors of the articles and by titles of the original journals) all the articles included in the reserve collection of journal articles.

Government publications Another collection deals with government publications, such as parliamentary papers, recurring statistical publications, and the published indexes.

Local collections Certain libraries may also carry local collections specializing in rare and antiquarian works or special interest titles relating to a specific geographical area or community.

Recreational collections Besides, municipal and some academic libraries are now keeping recreational collections of up-to-date paperbacks representing fiction of various kinds, in addition to selections of non-fiction works on travel, sports, games, cookery, philately, etc. Consult the library staff about the rules for using this collection, if one such exists in your library.

Aids to extend your search Further library aids may enable you to extend your search for information beyond your institutional or municipal library. These include the published catalogues of certain other libraries (such as the British Library in London); collections of bibliographies, abstracts and indexes; and access to on-line bibliographic and documentary data bases.

Databases and on-line searching Many libraries now, and the majority in the future, will have access to computerized data bases. These are computerized records on specific subjects. For instance, DIALOG comprises some 200 separate subject databases with divisions such as:

MEDLINE: dealing with medical matters
ERIC: educational research
FSTA: Food, Science and Technology

In this country there is BLAISE, which covers such files as Books in English.

Advantages There are several distinct advantages to this kind of on-line searching:

- *Speed.* The computer based indexes can perform very rapid searches indeed. Millions of records can be searched through in a matter of seconds.

- *Searching for relationships, contrasts or opposites.* This is where the computer search really comes into its own. The computer can handle disparate subjects, and can show possible interconnections and relationships by accessing a number of different records. For example, suppose you were interested in exploring aspects of language, artificial languages, and in particular, Esperanto (as in the sample essay in Chapter 11). You might want to see how many references there were in BLAISE to Esperanto (that would give you thousands of possible sources) and to dictionaries, which would narrow the search somewhat. If you were also interested in dictionaries in Esperanto published by UNESCO, then this is where the computer search would prove very useful indeed. In a matter of seconds you would be able to locate the references useful to your study.

- *Flexibility.* In addition to manipulating the search by subject, the computer can also be programmed to search for items by author, language and date.

- *Provision of hard copies.* Most databases now provide, at a cost, a printout service, on-line, at the library terminal from where the search is conducted. However, it is cheaper and more normal for copies of references to be printed off-line and posted to the library. Some databases also provide abstracts as well as references, but this is naturally more expensive.

Disadvantages

There are certain disadvantages to on-line searching:

- *Cost.* Searching is expensive. Charges range enormously, depending on the length of search and the database being interrogated. In the U.K., few searches are less than £10, many are more than £50.

- *Limitations.* Computerized databases are very dependent on the quality of the abstractors and indexers, and the width and topicality of the subject coverage. It is very important to recognize that databases cannot discriminate between the merits of individual references. If you have only one reference, such as Esperanto in the previous example, then you would be far better conducting an ordinary search through existing catalogues, abstract journals, encyclopaedias, etc. Remember also that there is no one database which will cover all your needs; you will have to locate which databases to interrogate. This brings us to the subject of keywords.

Keywords

If you turn to the sample report in Chapter 12, you will see how the student has written down the 'keywords' in his report. The keywords are the ones that will 'unlock' the search for references; they are the starting point for your enquiry. The clearer you are on which key terms you require further information, then the better the library staff will be able to help you with your search. There is no point in being vague. For instance, the student who comes up with the keyword 'Pressure' will only gain a mass of references covering such aspects as air-cabin pressure, tyre pressures, underwater pressures, etc. This particular student wanted information on muscle pressure!

Be certain what you want out of your search. Be certain that it is the kind of search that can best be done on computer. Finally ask your library staff for their advice.

Inter-Library Loan, photocopying

If you need a particular book or journal not stocked in the library, it may be borrowed for you from another library through the Inter-Library Loan network. Most libraries also provide a photocopying service at reasonable rates per page. The work to be photocopied must be permissible within the terms of the Copyright Act, and you are well advised to enquire of the library staff what the terms of this Act are.

A library is always changing

The more you use your library and avail yourself of its services and facilities, the easier and more efficient your research procedures will become. But a library is always changing — books and journals are added, others are discarded, and new and more advanced technological devices are being introduced into library operations to help you pursue your work more effectively. It is your responsibility to keep up with the changes. Some libraries will issue handouts to inform you of the workings of the particular library, and to describe the innovations in their services and facilities.

The library can in many ways be regarded as the 'brains' of your institution, because it is where all the knowledge and information are stored. Your task as a student on a research project is to know how to tap that storehouse of knowledge and information and to use it to your own best advantage.

SUMMARIZING

When you are retrieving information from printed sources, it is useful to know how to summarize an article, a chapter of a textbook, or a series of lecture notes. Here is an effective procedure to follow:

Pick out main points

Pick out the author's main points. Don't just copy them down but, as in all summary writing, put them in your own words. By doing so, you become more actively involved in the learning process, and the facts and ideas are more likely to stay with you.

Don't waste your time writing full sentences. Note only the key words and phrases. Use abbreviations whenever possible. You can always join up your notes into a completed summary later, if you wish.

With certain types of technical texts, you can probably make an adequate summary by using such visuals as diagrams, charts, tables or sketches, labelling them with key terms. See Chapter 10.

Example

As an example of the summarizing procedure, here is an original text in geology, followed by summary notes on it:

> In volcanoes of all kinds, the eventual extinction of the volcano itself and the complete freezing up of the vent follow the periods of explosion and discharge of lava. Even so, a great deal of heat in the solidifying magma still underlies the vent area. Before the final cooling and solidification can occur, this residual heat must escape to the surface. Thus, many residual heat phenomena are visible at the surface in the immediate vicinity of the extinct volcano. Gases of some of the more volatile substances, such as sulphur, borax and bismuth, as well as steam and carbon dioxide, escape through fissures in the shattered volcanic cone and the adjacent countryside. These places of escape, often open over many years, are called fumaroles, which may, in some cases, have economic value. For example, condensation sheds built over the fumaroles are used to collect sulphur, borax and other minerals. In Tuscany, Italy, fumaroles generate 30,000 horsepower, which is harnessed and transmitted for use in Pisa and Florence. Valuable mineral water is produced by water seeping through recent volcanic deposits and by water rising from the cooling magma. In Iceland and certain areas of New Zealand, mineral-free water, often discharged at a high temperature, is piped to the cities where it is used as a domestic hot water supply.   (218 words)
>
> John Vulcan, *Secrets of Volcanoes,* p. 58

Summary Notes

All volcanoes extinct after eruption. Vents freeze up.
Still heat under vent area — this must escape for cooling/hardening.
Residual heat from recently extinct volcanoes:
  — gases (sulph, borax, bismuth)
  — steam and CO_2

Fumaroles — vents where gases escape
Some economic value — collection of minerals
[e.g. Tuscany — elec. power generation
　— mineral water
Iceland & N.Z. — hot water piped for domestic use]

John Vulcan, *Secrets of Volcanoes,* p. 58

Notice that the examples are bracketed in the notes. Usually, in making a summary, you will not need the examples from the text, but sometimes a few examples help to fix an idea or a fact in your memory and provide you with material to back up general references.

A danger: distortion of ideas, data

One danger in summarizing another person's ideas or data is that, by reducing them, you might distort or oversimplify them. An example of this danger is seen in the first line of the summary notes. The original is:

In volcanoes of all kinds, the eventual extinction of the volcano itself and the complete freezing up of the vent follow the periods of explosion and discharge of lava. (29 words)

In the summary notes, this becomes:

All volcanoes extinct after eruption. Vents freeze up. (8 words)

Not all volcanoes are extinct, however. A more accurate summary note is:

In all volcanoes, period of eruption followed by extinction as vents freeze up. (13 words)

This version is five words longer than the first one, but it is truer to the author's statement in the original text. When you are summarizing another person's ideas or data, guard against 'editing out' key points just to reduce wordage. If you also alter the order of ideas in your summary, be careful that you don't produce a garbled or illogical text.

Abstracts

When you write a report, you may be required to include an abstract. This is a summary of all essential information contained in the report and must include keywords, which are necessary for access to databases. For an example of an abstract, see the sample report in Chapter 12.

Acknowledge sources

Always acknowledge the source of your text in your summary. Make a habit of noting down the author's name and the title of the work, which can be included in your bibliography if such is required, as in an essay or a technical report. It may also be necessary to note the page number or numbers for possible use in a footnote reference.

SUMMARY OF THE MAIN POINTS

■ Choose a topic, then decide on an aspect of it, or set up a practical hypothesis.

■ Information can be obtained from many sources, but most usually from a library.

■ Be systematic in taking notes.

■ Bibliographic entries are written according to standardized form, which may be established by departmental or institutional 'house styles'.

■ Become acquainted with the layout, services and facilities of your institutional or municipal library.

■ The card catalogue (author and subject) and the microfiche are the two main catalogues used in most up-to-date libraries.

■ The Universal Decimal Classification (UDC) is the generally used system to arrange the stock of books in a library (the Library of Congress system is also used in some cases).

■ Pick out the author's key words or phrases, and put them in your own words.

■ Diagrams and other visuals are often sufficient in summarizing technical texts.

■ Guard against distortion of ideas or data, and 'editing out' key points.

■ Acknowledge sources in summary notes.

Further Reading

Barrass, R.   *Scientists Must Write.*
                 Chapman and Hall, 1978.

Chapter 9 Organization of Material and Coherence in Writing

Seven methods to organize material

In this chapter, we will discuss seven methods of organizing material in your essay or report, namely:

1. logical
2. chronological
3. spatial
4. familiar-to-unfamiliar ordering
5. climactic ordering
6. anticlimactic ordering
7. whole-to-part/part-to-whole ordering

Six ways to ensure coherence

We will also consider six ways of ensuring coherence in your writing, by means of

1. consistent grammar
2. repetition
3. pronoun reference
4. chronological ordering of content in sentences
5. spatial structure
6. transition words

ORGANIZATION

What is logic?

Logic is correct reasoning. By means of logic we can find out what follows if we accept a given statement as true. A statement of fact is not logical or illogical in itself, although it can be true or false, or partly true and partly false. Only when a conclusion is drawn from a statement or statements does logic technically enter the process. Logic is the process of drawing a conclusion from one or more statements or propositions called premises.

Example: perfect syllogism

Here is an example of a perfectly true logical process, called a syllogism, in three parts: (A) major premise, (B) minor premise, and (C) conclusion:

(A) All men are mortal.

(B) John is a man.

∴ **(C)** John is mortal.

Logical fallacies

Perhaps Frank is one of the millionaires (and perhaps not).

Mistakes or fallacies occur when the conclusion, although logically correct in relation to the premises, is based on premises that are false. For example:

(A) All Americans are millionaires.

(B) Frank is an American.

∴ **(C)** Frank is a millionaire.

This is obviously untrue, for statistically not 'all' but only about 200,000 (or 'some') Americans are dollar millionaires. This is the fallacy of 'all and some', that is, 'all' is used ('All Americans are millionaires') when 'some' is meant. Logic alone is not always enough. Facts are needed as well. It would be factually true, and more logical, to say:

(A) Some Americans are millionaires.

(B) Frank is an American.

∴ **(C)** Perhaps Frank is one of the millionaires (and perhaps not).

Without more factual information about Frank's income, we cannot be more exact than this, but the conclusion is sufficiently qualified to ensure a certain measure of truthfulness, which ought to be generally acceptable.

Logical organization of material

When you organize your essay or report material logically, you must be sure that you have presented enough information to justify the conclusion you draw from it. Consider this sequence of statements:

(A) Sugar causes tooth decay.

(B) James likes sugar.

∴ **(C)** James has rotten teeth.

Let's analyse each part:

(A) 'Sugar causes tooth decay.' Although it used to be thought that starch caused tooth decay, dentists today attribute it to sugar in one's diet. So the major statement or premise can be accepted as true.

(B) 'James likes sugar.' Assuming this to be true, we cannot, however, know from this statement alone whether James eats enough sugar to cause tooth decay. We need more information, for example, what is James's sugar intake per day. There is a difference between liking sugar and eating excessive (or even small) quantities of it.

(C) Therefore, 'James has rotten teeth.' The 'therefore' leads to a very doubtful conclusion. Be careful when you use 'therefore' that you have adequately proved, demonstrated or explained your facts, so that your reader will understand the 'logic' of your conclusion. Just because James likes sugar does not necessarily mean that he has rotten teeth. He may, knowing the dangers of sugar intake, brush his teeth three times a day and visit his dentist for a checkup twice a year, and thus prevent tooth decay.

Example: improved
syllogism

To improve the accuracy of the sequence, we might rephrase the statements as follows:

(A) Sugar causes tooth decay.

(B) James likes sugar.

∴ **(C)** James will probably have rotten teeth unless he reduces his sugar intake and maintains his dental health.

The sequence is longer, but the conclusion is also closer to what is probably a truer statement of the facts.

Deductive reasoning

In logic, there are two methods of reasoning: the deductive and the inductive. When you use the deductive method, you proceed from the general statement (thesis) to the particular details and illustrations, for instance:

<u>Sugar is harmful to one's teeth.</u>   thesis statement
It attacks the enamel, and encourages the formation of plaque which in turn causes further } particular details
bacteria to attack the teeth.

In deductive reasoning, you have already researched the details and reached a conclusion, which is represented by the thesis statement. You may also use the deductive reasoning method in constructing all the paragraphs which comprise your essay or report, as in Fig. 1 (p. 82).

Inductive reasoning

When you use the inductive method, you proceed from particular details to a general statement based on them, with the thesis serving as a conclusion. Consider the reasoning used in constructing this paragraph:

In those countries, particularly in the Third World, where as yet there is very little intake of sugar, dental caries is almost unknown. True, there are many specific disorders of the gums and much in the way of broken or ill-formed teeth. But the lack of sugar, together with much chewing of meat, vegetables and nuts, makes the general dental condition far superior to that found in countries of the affluent North and West, where the consumption of sugar in the form of sweets and cakes is increasing year by year. Many detailed tests have been conducted on children's teeth in the U.K. (B.D.A., 1979). It has been shown conclusively that those children who have less sugar in their diet have less caries and stronger, healthier teeth. From this evidence, and from studies made in the Third World (W.H.O., 1981), we can safely assume that sugar in diet is the principal cause of rotten teeth.

The inductive method may be used in constructing and writing an essay or a report, where you first gather the details and then reach a general conclusion based on them. A diagram of the inductive method is shown in Fig. 2 (p. 83).

Whether you use the deductive or the inductive method, or, as is likely, both methods in combination, you must make sure that the logic of your writing is clear and correct. For instance, when you write up your lab report or notes on scientific experiments, you must show the proof to support the conclusions you reach, as here:

DEDUCTIVE METHOD

ESSAY
Introduction — **THESIS STATEMENT**
PARTICULARS
Paragraph 1 — **TOPIC SENTENCE**
PARTICULARS
Paragraph 2 — **TOPIC SENTENCE**
PARTICULARS
Paragraph 3 — **TOPIC SENTENCE**
PARTICULARS
Conclusion — **CONCLUDING STATEMENT**

Fig. 1   Diagram of deductive method in an essay or report (see p. 81)

On the substance X, test A was done which proved positive.

On the substance X, test B was done which proved positive.

On the evidence so far presented, a further test was done, which proved positive.

As a result of these tests, it is concluded that substance X is safe to use.

If you omit one of the tests, the conclusion is likely to be unsound. In writing an essay or a report, too, you must clearly lay out the structure of your material by one or more of the several methods of organization we are discussing. Otherwise, the structure of your essay or report may be too weak to support your argument.

INDUCTIVE METHOD

ESSAY		

Introduction	INTRODUCTION	
	PARTICULARS/EXAMPLES	
	THESIS STATEMENT	
Paragraph 1	EXAMPLES/REFERENCES	
	SECOND CONCLUDING STATEMENT	
Paragraph 2	PARTICULARS	
	THIRD CONCLUDING STATEMENT	
Paragraph 3	PARTICULARS	
	FOURTH CONCLUDING STATEMENT	
Conclusion	CONCLUSION	

Fig. 2   Diagram of inductive method in an essay or report (see p. 81)

Chronological ordering

Apart from the deductive and inductive methods, there are other ways of ordering your ideas and organizing your material in an essay or a report. One of the most common ways is chronological, that is, presenting events, stages of development, etc., in the order of their occurrence in time, as in the steps of a process, a biography, or a history. This structure can be useful when, introducing a subject, you relate how discoveries were made or theories developed over a period of time. For instance, on the subject of tooth decay, the writer might briefly discuss earlier theories of how dental caries is caused, from the starch theory up to present-day thinking, before developing the main body of the essay.

Spatial ordering

Another way to arrange information is in a spatial order, for instance, from top to bottom, north to south, east to west, home to abroad, earth to solar system to universe. This method is useful in writing on geographical subjects, but it may also be applied to good effect in other subjects where descriptions of places and physical directions are involved. For example, in the paragraph on tooth decay, the subject was

Familiar-to-unfamiliar ordering.

first mentioned in connection with the Third World (i.e., South and East), in comparison with the situation in the affluent North and West.

Familiar-to-unfamiliar ordering

The ordering of material from that which is familiar to the reader or listener to that which is unfamiliar is a basic structure used in almost all communication. In an essay or a speech, you usually start with information that is already known, to gain your reader's or listener's attention and interest, and then gradually introduce information that you believe the reader or listener will find new and perhaps difficult. By doing this, you will enlarge your reader's or listener's knowledge and understanding, which will be firmly grounded on what he or she already knows.

Climactic, anticlimactic ordering

This method of structuring material — climactic and anticlimactic — is used to present information or events in order of increasing or decreasing importance. For example, you might use the order of increasing importance in describing a series of historical events which came to a climax in a declaration of war, or in the rise to power of such a person as Napoleon. In anticlimactic ordering, the most important ideas or events are presented first, the least important ones being placed at the end of the sequence. For instance, in writing an essay on mountains, you might want to list a dozen or so peaks by height, starting with Mount Everest and concluding with one only a quarter as high.

Whole-to-part, part-to-whole ordering

By ordering material from the whole to part or the part to whole, you lead the reader from an overview of the complete subject to a consideration of its separate components, or, conversely, from the

Part-to-whole ordering.

separate components to the general subject. For instance, in an essay on chemistry, you might first present a general definition of chemistry and

then deal in detail with the sub-divisions of organic, inorganic and physical chemistry. As an example of ordering from the separate unit to the general subject, you might start your essay by discussing the instruments which comprise a modern symphony orchestra and conclude with a statement on the total effect created by these instruments playing together in harmony.

COHERENCE

Coherence must exist in your writing itself as well as in the various methods you may use in structuring the material in your essay or report. Coherence (from the Latin *cohaerere*, to stick) means a sticking or holding together, consistency. In writing, coherence means sticking to the lines of your argument. This can be achieved in several ways.

Consistent grammar

One way to achieve coherence in writing is through consistent grammar. Consider this paragraph:

A period of probation on the city streets is a wonderful education for any young police recruit. The city is full of tests of nerve and resolve. You cannot imagine how difficult it is to remember all that you were told about the law when you are suddenly presented with an accident on the street. Accidents will suddenly happen. Criminals will not wait until you have consulted your police handbook. Previous to recent reform, police on probation were expected to learn as they went along. Now they will have to act on their own initiative. Police work is becoming more and more difficult, and the need is great for talented and intelligent police recruits.

This passage lacks coherence. The underlined topic sentence sets a course which the subsequent sentences do not follow. The subjects of the sentences change from 'period of probation' to 'the city' to 'you' to 'accidents' to 'criminals' to 'police work'. The tenses change, too, from the present of '*is* a wonderful education' to the future of 'accidents *will* suddenly happen' to the past of 'police on probation *were* expected'.

Unity

Examine the redraft of this paragraph below, noticing how unity is created by coherence of subject matter and grammatical structure:

> A period of probation on the city streets is a wonderful education for young police <u>recruits</u>. <u>They</u> will be fully tested by the demands of law enforcement in the city and by having to apply lectures on law to the handling of accidents in the street. Nor will <u>recruits</u> have time to consult <u>their</u> police handbooks while criminals obligingly wait. <u>They</u> will not have time to learn so much on the job either. <u>They</u> will be expected to act on <u>their</u> own initiative. The demand is for talented and intelligent <u>recruits</u> to measure up to the demands of a police force facing more and more difficult challenges.

In this version of the paragraph, the sentences do not jump from idea to idea as in the first draft. The idea stated in the topic sentence, referring to the education of young police recruits, is developed consistently throughout, and the tenses are more consistent, too.

Repetition

Another way of achieving coherence in your writing is by the repetition of key words, such as the word 'recruits' in the above paragraph. Here is a second example, in which the repeated words are underlined:

> <u>Alarm clocks</u> are, understandably, the most abused of all timepieces. Memories of shrill bells are hardly likely to endear them to anyone. Even so, most of us need an <u>alarm clock</u> to waken us in the morning. Some <u>alarm clocks</u> are difficult to read. Make sure that the <u>clock face</u> is easy to see in the dark and that the <u>alarm</u> is loud enough to be effective.

Pronoun reference

The repetition of the words 'alarm' and 'clocks' gives coherence to the writing. But overuse of a particular word or of a group of words can result in the reader becoming bored or irritated with your style. Pronoun reference is a way to avoid over-repetition and achieve the same coherence, as in this example, in which the pronoun 'it' refers to 'alarm clock' throughout:

> The <u>alarm clock</u> is, basically, a very simple device, and so, in order to boost sales, manufacturers have tried to make <u>it</u> a more interesting commodity. They have added certain extras to <u>it</u>. Tea-making facilities provide you with a cup of tea when you wake up. Radios switch on when you switch <u>it</u> off. Telephone recording devices inform you of calls you missed during the night. <u>It</u> is no longer a simple device with a horrible sound that you switch off, but a complicated product of the computer age.

Chronological ordering

Just as the material of a whole essay or report can be ordered chronologically, so can the sentences in a paragraph, when the topic permits, as in this example:

> Three months before a major competition the athletes will begin to get themselves into the best possible physical and mental shape, by work outs and road running. Two months before the games they will engage in serious track practice. About three weeks before the big event, they will make time trials with other experienced runners. On the day of the games, they are fully prepared to compete.

The paragraph is structured in descending chronological order, from earliest to most recent times. Use this method only when it helps the reader's understanding of an event or a process.

Spatial ordering

Spatial ordering can be used effectively in writing where, for instance, the description of movement is essential to the reader's ability to visualize a scene, as in this example:

> If we look at the outside of the building first, we see with what care the builders have massed the enormous marble slabs to create the effect of broad faces and buttresses. On entering the building, we are struck by the height of the beamed ceiling, the effect of space created by the gothic archways. Now walking up to the altar, we can see the extraordinary craftsmanship that created the wooden screen. Standing in front of the altar itself, we are impressed by its simplicity and size, supporting a tall crucifix carved in teak.

This method of organizing information is useful in describing an operation or a procedure, or in comparing one structure or layout with another.

Transition words and phrases

Transition words and phrases are those which indicate comparison, contrast, alternatives and results. Among the most commonly used are 'but', 'however', 'therefore', 'consequently', 'on the other hand', and 'as a result'. For example:

> The building was ancient but its interior was ultra-modern.

> The building was ancient and the stone work was beginning to crumble. However, inside everything was in a modern style and in good repair.

Both within the sentence, as in the first example, and between two sentences, as in the second, coherence is obtained by the use of transition words showing contrast.

Such transition words as 'therefore' and 'consequently' indicate logical relationships. Use these words carefully, and be sure that the logical relationship is clear, as it is *not* in this example:

> This building is very old, therefore it must be preserved.

The transition word 'therefore' is not followed by a logical conclusion drawn from the evidence given to the reader in the first part of the sentence. Because a building is very old does not necessarily mean that it should be preserved in all circumstances. In this second example, the use of 'therefore' is justified:

> This building is very old and the only one of its kind in existence. Therefore it should be preserved.

Sometimes we use transition words and phrases without thinking what they mean. For example:

> Crime is on the increase, as a result of which more and more criminals are being sent to prison. Consequently, more of our tax money has to be spent on providing roofs over the heads of the nation's wrongdoers.

Several assumptions have been made in this passage and presented as firm conclusions:

> **(A)** Crime is on the increase.
>
> **(B)** More and more criminals are being sent to prison.
>
> ∴ **(C)** More taxes are spent on criminals' accommodation.

Each of these three assumptions needs more clarification and supporting evidence before the conclusion can be accepted as valid. It is difficult to say whether crime is on the increase or not, because much depends on how each crime is defined and recorded, and on how crime statistics are compiled and by whom.

In this chapter, in which we have examined some of the elements of logical writing and methods of organizing material, the key points to remember are:

- Keep your reader always in mind.
- Do not make any assumptions.

What appears straightforward and logical to you may seem confused and illogical to your reader.

Before submitting your essay or report, check it to see that you have backed up your statements with hard evidence and that you have referred to the sources of your material.

If you use the deductive method, make sure that your general thesis is supported by subsequent particulars. If you use the inductive method, make sure that you have presented enough particulars on which to base your general conclusion. In practice, you will probably use a combination of both methods in developing the logical structure of your essay or report. Be careful, too, how you use 'therefore', 'as a result', 'consequently', and other transition words and phrases.

SUMMARY OF THE MAIN POINTS

- The seven main methods of organizing material are:
  1. logical
  2. chronological
  3. spatial
  4. familiar-to-unfamiliar ordering
  5. climactic ordering
  6. anticlimactic ordering
  7. whole-to-part/part-to-whole ordering
- Six ways to ensure coherence in writing are:
  1. consistent grammar
  2. repetition
  3. pronoun reference
  4. chronological ordering of content in sentences
  5. spatial structure
  6. transition words
- Logic is correct reasoning, demonstrated by use of major and minor premises and a conclusion.
- Logical fallacies occur when the conclusion does not follow from the premises, one of which is faulty in some way.
- Deductive reasoning starts with a general thesis statement and follows it with particulars.
- Inductive reasoning starts with particulars and arrives at a concluding general thesis statement based on them.

Further Reading

Jepson, R.W.   *Teach Yourself to Think.*
                      The English Universities Press Ltd., 1963.

Mander, A.E.   *Clearer Thinking (Logic for Everyman).*
                      Watts & Co., 1936.

Thouless, Robert H.   *Straight and Crooked Thinking,*
                      revised and enlarged edition. Pan, 1971.

Turk, C. and   *Effective Writing.*
J. Kirkman.   E. & F.N. Spoon, 1982.

Chapter 10 Graphs, Charts, Diagrams, Tables

In this chapter, we will deal with some means of communication which are primarily visual. Among these means are:

- graphs
- charts
- diagrams
- tables

72 hours after the lecture...

Below are examples of ways in which these means can be used to convey information, by converting words and figures into 'visuals' of one kind or another.

Our experience is that after listening to an hour's lecture, students begin very rapidly to forget the information given them. Twenty-four hours after the lecture, most of the students will have forgotten 75% of the information. After forty-eight hours, the amount the students remember has usually sunk to 15%. Yet if the students review the information by noting the key points in the first place and then reading over or discussing or using their notes, the retention levels are as high as 70-85%.

Above we have presented these findings in words and numerals. Let's put these findings into graph form, so that you can 'see' them better.

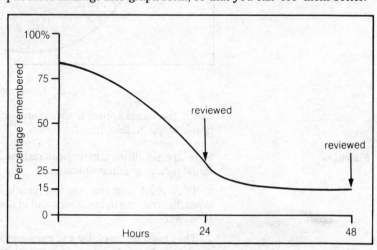

Fig. 1   Typical graph

The impact of the visual presentation is greater than the combination of words and percentages. You are likely to understand the information more quickly and remember it longer.

Here is a second example.

Let's suppose that in a recent survey of managers in the retail sector, it was found that their day was divided roughly into the following segments:

- talking and interviewing, 40%

- writing, 10%

- answering the telephone and making calls, 15%

- reading, especially reports and memos, 25%

- visits, meals, entertaining, etc., 10%

Compare this verbal and numerical presentation of the information with its treatment in a pie chart:

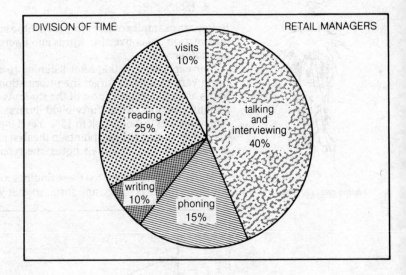

Fig. 2   Typical pie chart

Again, the visual appeal is strong and vivid. Because it is, the information is easier to take in.

Six rules

Here are six important considerations to keep in mind when using visual means of communication:

1. They must help the communication process, not hinder it. Sometimes illustrations in textbooks and in speeches only confuse the reader or viewer.

2. They must be carefully and purposefully slotted into the text or talk, not just put in at random. It is pointless, for instance, to have a page showing a chart which does not relate to the text.

3. Do not assume that your audience will know as much about your visual presentation as you do. For instance, because you know what, in economics,

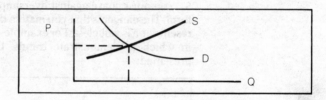

Fig. 3   Typical inadequate graph

means, do not take it for granted that others looking at this graph will also understand it. You may have to add more detail and reference, as in this version:

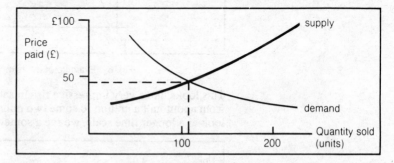

Fig. 4   Revised, more detailed graph

4. You must always tell your audience the source of the information in the graph, the chart, the map, etc. In a written text, unless the supplementary item is original with you, you should document the source in a footnote, and also enter the source in the bibliography at the end of the text, as in this instance:

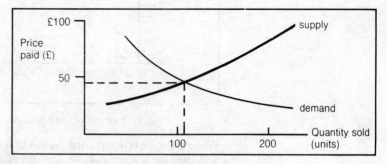

Fig. 5[1]   Example of footnoted graph

The footnote on this would be:

1 Paul Smith and John Jones, *Basic Economics,* p. 90.

The bibliographic entry would be:

Smith, Paul and John Jones. *Basic Economics.*
London: Hardly Press, 1979.

5. You must guard against oversimplifying your information in graph form. The danger is that you may so distort the true picture that the representation is valueless. For example, when selecting a given time period in which to demonstrate trends, be careful how these trends are presented:

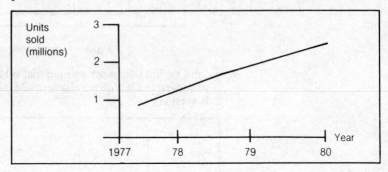

Fig. 6   Example of oversimplified graph

This looks like a very impressive rise in sales between 1977 and 1980, from about half a million to some two million units sold. But when we look at a longer time scale, we see a somewhat different picture:

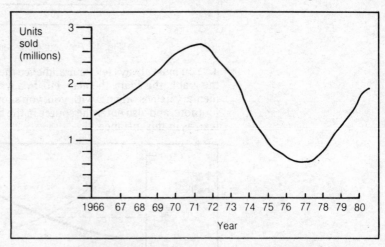

Fig. 7   Example of more detailed, more accurate graph

When the scale is lengthened, we see that sales between the years 1977 and 1980 are not spectacular. Compared with the mid and late sixties, the sales are disappointing.

6. Do not confuse the reader or viewer by overloading one chart, graph or map with information. For instance, when you try to plot a number of different variables on a single chart to make your point, as in Fig. 8, you may so bewilder the reader or viewer that the point of the graph is lost. In this case, it would be better to present two separate charts: one showing wages and unit costs, the other sales and dividends. Colour can be helpful, too, in making your illustrations more 'visible', but colour ought not to distract the viewer from the facts or relationships which you are trying to illustrate.

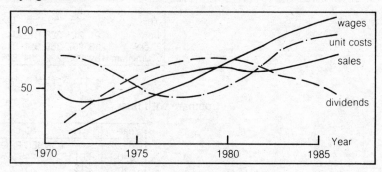

Fig. 8   Example of overloaded chart

Here are some different types of display which are commonly used:

Tables

The purpose of a table is to give the reader numerical information at a glance. But if the numbers are hard to see and difficult to interpret, the table may interfere with one's reading rather than help clarify an aspect of the text. Let's examine this table:

Thousands	1960	1970	1980
Total employed	339.9	558.7	621.7
Males	130.0	224.2	301.6
Females	209.9	334.5	320.5

Fig. 9   Example of crowded, unclear table

Do the figures stand out? What would the reader remember after turning the page? Let's improve the table by redesigning it, thus:

Thousands	1960	1970	1980
Total employed	340*	559	622
Females	210	334	320
Males	130	224	301

Numbers employed in French catering industry.
French Gov't Dept of Statistics 1982.
*Numbers rounded to nearest whole number.

Fig. 10   Example of redesigned table

Round up figures to the nearest whole number, as here: 339.9 becomes 340 (thousand). This is done to create better reader comprehension of the figures. Always tell the reader that you have rounded up the figures, and always keep for reference or place in an appendix to the text the complete figures to several decimal places. Otherwise, you might be suspected of 'massaging' the figures to your own advantage.

Use column rather than row layout. In the first version of the table (Fig. 9), the figures were cramped. They were not carefully lined up and there was no compartment separating the explanation (total employed) from the subsequent figures. Set out the data in a visually attractive manner. It is easier to read information in vertical columns than in horizontal rows. Avoid this kind of presentation:

Year	'40	'45	'50	'55	'60	'65	'70	'75	'80
Iron	201	213	228	312	345	368	423	432	398
Steel	245	267	289	321	346	389	398	413	400
Aluminium	189	200	222	234	245	256	267	278	289

Fig. 11   Typical horizontal table

Compare with this:

Year	Iron	Steel	Aluminium
	TONNES PRODUCED		
1940	201	245	189
'45	213	267	200
'50	228	289	222
'55	312	321	234
'60	345	346	245
'65	368	389	256
'70	423	398	267
'75	432	413	278
'80	398	400	289

Fig. 12   Typical vertical table

In this arrangement, it is easier to spot variations. For instance, in the second version (Fig. 12), the decline in the production of steel between 1975 and 1980 becomes more apparent than it was when the data were set out in rows. It is easier to look down than along a line of figures.

Other ways to highlight variation

Other ways of highlighting variation in a table of figures are by underlining individual figures, placing asterisks (*) at them or putting them in heavy (bold) print.

Bar charts

Much information can also be put into bar charts. They consist of rectangles or straight lines drawn to a common scale and lengths which represent the quantities to be displayed. You can display the information on how managers' time was spent during a typical working day in a vertical bar chart, instead of a pie chart as in Fig. 2:

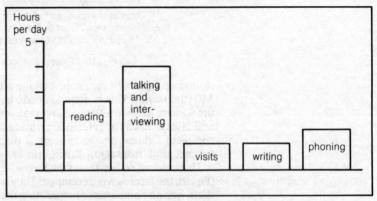

Fig. 13   Example of vertical bar chart

or in a horizontal bar chart:

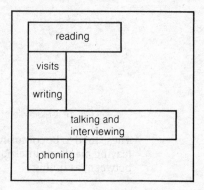

Fig. 14   Example of horizontal bar chart

The main advantage of bar charts is that comparisons between one element of information and another are immediately seen.

Composite or component bar charts

If you have a great deal of information to put on a chart, you can use the composite or component bar chart. Suppose you wish to compare the different working practices of a number of different managers from different sectors of the retail trade. You can use a vertical bar chart but divide the column into different components to indicate the different sectors, as here:

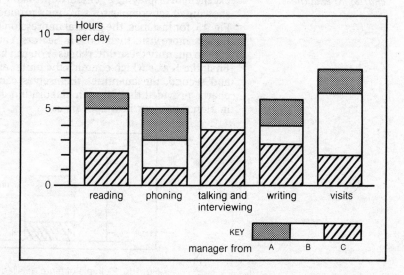

Fig. 15   Example of compound or composite bar chart

Colour and shading

The aim here is to show the comparisons quickly. You must supply a key to the different colours or patterns of shading. Avoid having similar colours or similar shading/stipple effects close together as in Fig. 16:

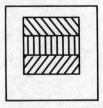

Fig. 16   Example of ill-distinguished colours or shading in chart

These tend to be confusing to the eye. Instead, break up the patterns by leaving blanks or interposing markedly different colours or shading in between, as in this:

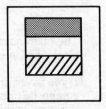

Fig. 17   Example of more easily distinguishable colours or shading in chart

Disadvantage of all charts: no exactness

One major disadvantage of all bar charts is that, although they are excellent in displaying a general impression, they are less satisfactory in showing exact comparisons in units produced, hours worked, etc. In Fig. 15, for instance, the general impression that managers from Sector B make more visits than those in Sectors A and C is present, but it is not easy to quantify these differences. You can help the reader in two ways. First, the X axis which contains the units can be more sharply defined, and second, the quantities themselves can be indicated on the bar charts, provided that all such elaboration does not obscure the information. The chart now appears as:

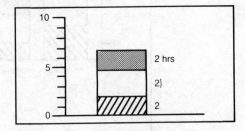

Fig. 18   Example of more detailed and exact chart

Histograms

A special form of bar chart, histograms display the frequency of occurrence of the subject under scrutiny within defined limits called class limits. For example, in a class of students, the marks obtained for a particular project could be expressed first as a table (see Fig. 19):

Marks obtained	Number of students awarded the marks
10-19	2
20-29	6
30-39	10
40-49	12
50-59	16
60-69	10
70-79	6
80-89	1
90-100	0

Fig. 19   Typical table

Then as a histogram:

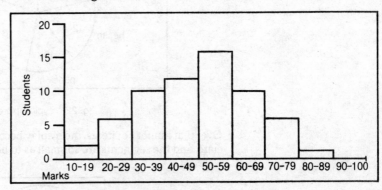

Fig. 20   Example of information presented as histogram,
showing frequency of occurrence

In the histogram, the pattern stands out more clearly than in the table. It is instantly apparent from this histogram that marks were bunched in the 49-59 range, while comparatively few came in the extremes.

Frequency polygons

In this slightly modified histogram, a dot is placed at the point where the top of each rectangle would be. Then the dots are joined up to form a continuous line. The students' marks now appear thus:

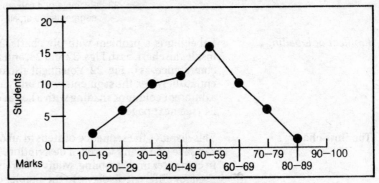

Fig. 21   Typical frequency polygon

Pie charts

Fig. 2 is an example of a pie chart. It consists of a circle divided pie-like into portions, each one in proportion to the size of the figure represented. The whole circle should equal 100%, although the segments can be expressed in units. Its main drawback is that it is useful only when you have a limited amount of information to convey.

If, for example, you wish to display how a certain country spent its money, you can, in a pie chart, adequately account for five or six items, as here (note that you should identify the units):

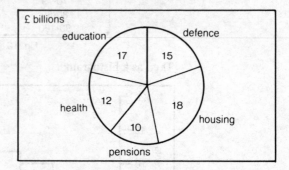

Fig. 22   Typical pie chart

Over that number of items, the display becomes more difficult to appreciate, and the segments are so small as to be useless, as in this example:

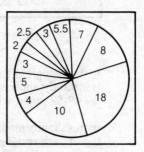

Fig. 23   Example of disadvantage of pie chart:
segments too small

Problem of labelling

Labelling is a problem with pie charts. You might write percentages inside the chart, as in Figs. 22 and 24, and label the items around the circumference, as in Fig. 22. You might also use colour or shading to differentiate between the segments, with units marked inside the circle, and in a different colour or shading with a key at one side of the chart, as in Fig. 24 (see next page).

The flow chart

This displays the sequence of steps in an operation. If it is well drawn, it can save you many words of description. You may already have used it in computer programming. Many different techniques and symbols are used for different displays. In the simpler charts, three symbols are used (see Fig. 25 on next page):

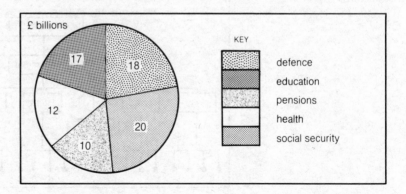

Fig. 24   Example of shaded pie chart with key

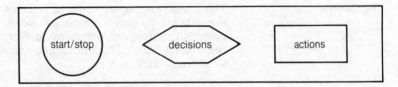

Fig. 25   Examples of flow chart symbols

A typical flow chart looks like this:

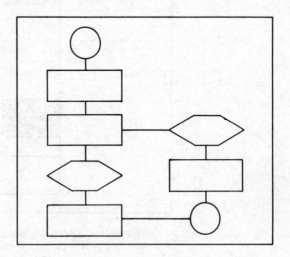

Fig. 26   Typical flow chart using three symbols

The organizational chart

This is a 'family tree' type display of organizational decision making and communications in diagrammatic form. For instance, the organization of your academic institution could be represented as in Fig. 27:

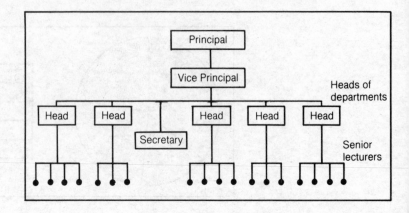

Fig. 27   Example of 'family tree' type of organizational chart

The Gantt chart

This is used to compare real achievements with planned performance. For instance, you might compare students' average numbers of essays, projects and other coursework assignments produced during their first two years in higher education with the number required in the coursework regulations, as here:

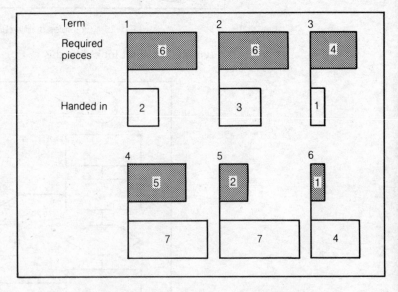

Fig. 28   Example of Gantt chart to compare real achievements with planned performance

Statistical maps

These are maps shaded or coloured, and labelled, to display statistical information in a spatial pattern. Such maps can be of a national or an international dimension. The one in Fig. 29 (see next page) shows the number of seats allotted to each of the EEC countries in the European Parliament at Strasbourg in 1985:

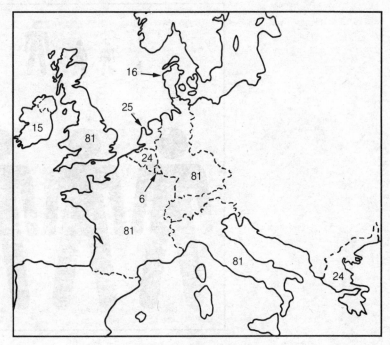

Fig. 29   Typical statistical map

If you are interested in showing spatial variations in geographical areas, this type of map can be very satisfactory.

Pictograms

In pictograms, figures are represented by pictures. Great care is needed in interpreting what they really mean, because it is easy to mislead the viewer with them. For instance, the total number of members of the EEC European Parliament could be listed by country, as here:

United Kingdom	81	Netherlands	25
West Germany	81	Greece	24
France	81	Belgium	24
Italy	81	Denmark	16
Luxembourg	6	Ireland	15

Fig. 30   Example of listed information

or more attractively (but misleadingly) shown in a pictogram, as in Fig. 31. The danger inherent in Fig. 31 is that the reader gets the impression of a far greater disparity between the countries than is in fact the case. This is because the figures are drawn to *heights* representing the numbers of seats held, but this makes the *areas* of the figures out of all proportion to the relative numbers of seats.

A far better way to present a pictogram is to use repeated little figures, each one representing a specified unit, as in Fig. 32:

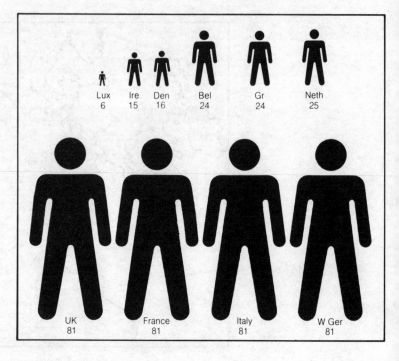

Fig. 31   Misleading pictogram

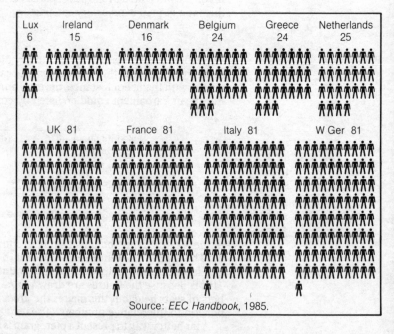

Source: *EEC Handbook*, 1985.

Fig. 32   Improved pictogram

If you use the pictogram, always include the exact numbers and the source of the data you have drawn upon to construct the display. Remember to interpret this type of statistical display with utmost caution.

SUMMARY OF THE MAIN POINTS

■ Place yourself in the reader's or viewer's position, and ask yourself: does this visual aid tell me anything that words could not do as well?

■ Keep the visuals clear.

■ Be bold and deliberate in your use of lettering, design and colour.

■ Don't misrepresent facts for the sake of simplification.

■ Always give the source of your data, placing it in a prominent position near the diagram.

■ Be sure you know what you are trying to provide with your visual aid: an explanation? an illustration? a dramatic representation?

■ Use words instead if you are unsure about your objective in using the visual aid.

Further Reading

Barrass, R.	*Scientists Must Write.* Chapman and Hall, 1978.
Panton, P.	*Communication Skills.* Hutchinson, 1980.
Woodward, J.F.	*Science in Industry, Science of Industry.* Aberdeen University Press, 1982.
Woolcott, L. and W. Unwin.	*Communication for Business and Secretarial Students.* Macmillan, 1979.

Chapter 11   The Essay

What is an essay?

An essay is an informal prose composition of varying length, in which the writer presents his or her knowledge of, and opinions about, a certain topic. We can identify four main types of essay:

- factual: e.g.,

  The history of town planning in the U.S.A.
- expository: e.g.,

  A personal view of town planning in the U.K.
- argumentative: e.g.,

  The case for and against town planning
- imaginative: e.g.,

  Town planning in Shangri-La

Students in the arts, humanities, social sciences, technology and pure sciences are required from time to time to submit essays, either in examinations or as part of coursework, or both, although these essays may be called projects, assessment exercises, or simply individual pieces of work, and they may run in length from a few hundred words to several thousand. But whatever the particulars of the essay, the principles of preparing and writing it remain the same.

The essay as test

The essay thus becomes a test of the student's ability

- to structure material in a limited period of time and within a limited number of words
- to write well under pressure, as in an examination

Writing well under pressure

- to produce within these limits well thought-out arguments, supported by evidence and references to sources
- to use language in a clear, logical manner in order to express ideas or present factual information

These skills come with much practice, but it is also necessary for the student to know what are the steps to take in writing the essay, and what are the ingredients of a good essay.

Four steps

The four steps to take in writing an essay are:

1. think about your topic, and note down facts and ideas as they come to you
2. construct an outline of your essay by arranging the facts and ideas under various sub-headings
3. write the essay
4. revise the text and proofread it

Ingredients of a good essay

The ingredients of a good essay are:

1. relevance of material
2. planning and organization of material
3. style of writing: clear, correct, concise and coherent
4. presentation of material in a neat, accessible layout

Relevance

Relevance of material in your essay is important, because the *lack* of it poses problems for those who read and grade your work. Irrelevancies usually occur when you do not answer the question set by the examiner, but they may also occur when you select your own topic. One way to

keep yourself from straying from the topic is to divide the title of the question into its component parts, and stick to them in your answer. For example, here is a question from a social-science question paper. The topic is selection interviewing.

> What are the main difficulties facing the interviewer in assessing candidates for employment? How can training in interview techniques help and what kind of training would you recommend? Give reasons.

Before writing a word of your essay answer, you will want at least to underline each component of the question, or, better, number each part as a sub-heading:

1. What are the main difficulties facing the interviewer in assessing candidates for employment?

   — enumerate difficulties

   — what are the standards of assessment?

   — what kind of candidates?

   — what kind of employment?

2. How can training in interviewing techniques help?

   — nature of training: where? with whom? facilities? duration?

   — what are the techniques being used? their degree of success?

3. What kind of training would you recommend?

   — depending on such factors as time, personnel, money, ability, purpose

4. Reasons for your recommendations

   — following from points under no. 3

Next decide how much space to devote to each part of the question, always taking into account your time and word limits. Don't begin writing the essay unless you are certain that you know what the question asks for, and what kind of information is required from you to answer it. If you stick to the points in your list of components, you are less likely to introduce irrelevant material into your essay.

Planning and organization

The planning and organization of essay material are closely related. They involve the structuring and arrangement of ideas and factual information. An essay without a solid structure sprawls, becoming a disjoined patchwork of words, which is difficult to read and to grade fairly, as it may have some excellent ideas or interesting information in it. To achieve this solid structure, you must plan your essay and organize your material in advance, perhaps working out a paragraph by paragraph, item by item approach.

Basic structure

The basic structure that every essay should have is:

- beginning: introduction
- middle: development
- end: conclusion

Types of organization

There are also several basic types of organization of material:

- chronological: for biographical and historical topics
- logical: for topics requiring argument or development of ideas
- alphabetical or numerical: for listing certain kinds of items, e.g., persons, quantities of goods
- spatial: for deploying diagrams, maps, charts, graphs, etc., in an essay
- degree of size or importance: for itemization, e.g., listing mountains by height

You may, of course, wish to use two or more of these organizational methods in one essay, depending on the kind and scope of the topic.

THE EXAM ESSAY

Planning an exam essay

In planning an examination essay, you must devise a method that is practical to apply within the given time and word limits.

Gather ideas

First, you must gather your ideas. Put these down on paper, in any order, as they occur to you. The more ideas you have, the more you can select from when you start to write. Ideas will also occur to you as you write, and these may be included or rejected according to the needs of your overall plan.

Select ideas

Next, you will select your ideas and start arranging them in order by one or more of the organizational methods already mentioned. Delete irrelevant ideas. Place the remaining ones into paragraph groupings under sub-headings. Isolate those ideas which will serve as useful introductory points. At this stage in your planning, don't worry about a conclusion. If you have planned your essay well, and organized the material according to some definite method or methods, your conclusion ought to follow logically from the preceding paragraphs of the essay.

Sample exam question

To illustrate this planning technique, we will consider how a student of economics organized his material for a first-year examination essay. The question was:

> 'The market price of any factor of production is determined by supply and demand.' Briefly explain this statement and discuss its relevance to the ways in which wages are determined in modern industrial society.

Separation of question

This is a complex question, and before the student could attempt to answer it, he had to separate it into two parts:

1. Briefly explain the quoted statement.
2. Discuss its relevance to the ways in which wages are determined in modern industrial society.

Gathering ideas

He then started gathering ideas in a general way:

- simple supply-and-demand theory
- too simple for wages, except in cases of footballers, pop singers

- factors in determining wages:
    - public sector, Govt limits on wages
    - relativity and union action
    - labour laws; equal payment
    - machinery and automation, labour replacement
    - taxes, collective bargaining
    - levels of employment
    - overseas competition
- examples:
    - shipbuilding
    - car industry policy (Ford)
    - teachers' unions
    - policy of employers' organizations

Organizing ideas

Next, the student sorted these ideas into a logical structure, with a beginning (introduction), middle (development), and end (conclusion):

A. Introduction:
  - simple supply-and-demand theory is fine,
    but in practice . . .
  - it's too simple for wages, especially with trade unions,
    except in cases of footballers and pop singers, who
    respond to real supply and demand

B. Development, with paragraph numbers:
  1. collective bargaining; e.g., teachers
  2. size of public sectors
  3. relativity; carry-over from one industry to another
  4. incomes policy: Govt attempts, failures
  5. labour laws; redundancy payments, etc.
  6. tax effects on take-home pay
  7. replacement of labour by automation (employers' policy)
  8. levels of employment
  9. overseas competition (shipbuilding)

C. Conclusion:
  - Although supply and demand theory does not have a large role
    to play in deciding the level of wages, it does affect a number
    of jobs in industry.

Using such a detailed, carefully planned and organized outline, the student had little trouble in completing his essay with relevant information, examples, and facts.

Style

Style — the way in which the essay is written — must also be considered. To some extent, every writer has his or her own style, a personal way of self-expression. When writing an essay, however, you will want to cultivate an impersonal style, as well as paying attention to grammar, punctuation and spelling. Generally speaking, your essay style should have the following qualities:

- clarity of expression: words must be chosen carefully, their meaning(s) fully understood
- correctness in grammar, punctuation and spelling
- coherence in sentence structure and development of ideas
- conciseness in choice and use of vocabulary
- standard English vocabulary: slang and colloquial expressions are best avoided except in quotations or in making a special point using inverted commas around the words
- objectivity: if the topic is being treated impersonally, do not use such expressions as 'I think', 'in my opinion', 'I believe', unless you are invited to give a personal opinion (see Chapter 12, 'Use of passive voice').

Paragraphs

As for paragraphs, don't number them in the general essay, although you should do so in a technical report. You should also avoid using the very short, snappy, single-sentence paragraph, which is acceptable in certain types of journalism, but out of place in an essay where you are interested in developing ideas more fully.

The opening and closing sentences of each paragraph should be carefully considered and constructed. By keeping a principal idea in mind throughout your essay, you will be able to compose a unified structure, instead of a series of disconnected fragments.

Introductory paragraph

The introductory paragraph requires considerable thought. It should attract and hold the reader's attention, perhaps with a striking or witty first sentence, or a relevant anecdote, or a general observation relating to the topic, or even a definition of terms if this is necessary. Whichever device is used, the reader should know at once what the topic of the essay is, even if the title also announces it clearly enough. A good title

Grabbing the reader's attention

identifies the topic in a few words, and may suggest an attitude or a point of view, or pose a question to be answered.

Final paragraph

The final paragraph must likewise be given serious thought. Your essay should not just stop. The reader should feel that your essay has been properly completed. The conclusion of your essay may be a summary of arguments and a restatement of findings, or a generalization based on the facts presented, or recommendations if these are called for, or an apt quotation from some appropriate source. The kind of final paragraph you write will be determined to a large extent by the kind of essay you have written, but it should relate, one way or another, to what has gone before. In writing the opening sentence of the final paragraph, avoid such over-used phrases as 'In conclusion', 'To sum up', 'Finally', and 'In the last analysis'. Try to be a little more original!

THE COURSEWORK ESSAY

Planning a coursework essay

When you plan a coursework essay, you will have more time and more words assigned, as well as greater opportunity to organize your material, and to refer to lecture notes, books, and other sources. See also Chapter 8, and Chapter 9, 'Organization'.

The general and the particular aspect

A first-year student of English chose the title 'An International Language' for her topic. In general, she wanted to cover artificially created languages, and, in particular, the competition to them from English as a world language. It is necessary for a student to know which aspect or limited area of the general topic to tackle in an essay. Unless the aspect or area is chosen with care, the task of research will become unmanageable (see Chapter 8, 'Finding an aspect').

Spider web no. 1

First, using the spider-web method, she sketched in the general areas to be covered in her essay. She preferred this method to the list, as was used in preparing the economics examination essay, because it enabled her to see inter-relationships better, and to appreciate where the gaps were in her knowledge which had to be filled in from her reading and research.

The first sketch of her spider web looked like this:

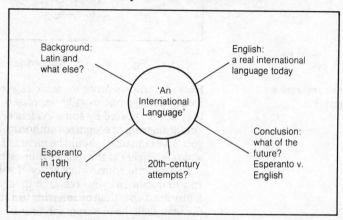

Fig. 1   Preliminary spider-web layout

Gathering material

Following the bare suggestions and queries, she started to gather her material from authoritative sources on the subject, which she appended to her essay as the bibliography. With this greater knowledge, she was ready to enlarge her spider web to draw in links between the separate areas, and to number the areas in chronological order, because this is a topic dealing with developments over a period of time. (For a full exposition of the spider-web technique, we recommend you read Tony Buzan's book, *Use Your Head;* see Further Reading.)

Spider web no. 2

Her second version of the spider web looked like this:

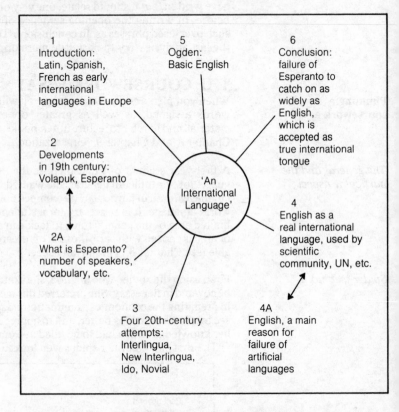

Fig. 2   More detailed and developed spider-web layout

Use of reference material

How do you incorporate your reference material into your essay? Examiners are not usually impressed with general statements unless they are supported by some evidence, such as a survey, statistics, or a quotation from a recognized authority. The textbooks and other sources you have consulted should be included in a bibliography (a list of books and references) at the end of your essay.

In a general coursework essay, it will probably not be necessary for you to document your research in any more detail, for example, with footnotes, other than by referring to a source by author or title or both in the text itself, as in paragraph four of 'An International Language'.

While conducting your research, you should always note down the basic facts about the sources you are reading, namely: author, title, publisher and date of publication for a book; and author, title of article, title of magazine, serial numbers (if any) and date of publication for a magazine; plus page numbers for quotations and borrowed facts and figures. If your quotations, facts and figures can be readily verified, your essay will gain in authenticity and authoritativeness.

Layout

The appearance of your essay is also worth consideration. A sloppy, much-blotted paper is offensive to look at and will probably be difficult to read. Adopt a uniform and consistent layout in which to present your material. Your examiner will be grateful to you for making your essay easier, and more enjoyable, to read. For a simple, yet comprehensive and attractive layout, we suggest the following points:

- a $1\frac{1}{2}''$ (4 cm) margin all round the text on each page, which helps the reader focus his attention on the writing and leaves him or her space in which to write comments and corrections

- standard A4 wide-lined paper if you are writing by hand, or plain A4 if you are typing; use one side of the paper only, and double-space all typing

- pages numbered in an immediately visible place, for instance, in the upper right-hand corner of each page

- pages paper-clipped or stapled together

- blottings and other mistakes eliminated with correction fluid

- a title page bearing certain basic facts that any reader might need to know to write a bibliographic entry on your essay:

  — name of your institution

  — name of department assigning essay

  — course title

  — title of your essay

  — your name as author of essay

  — your course and year

  — name of lecturer to whom essay is submitted, e.g., 'Submitted to John Smith'

  — date essay is submitted

Paragraph outline

Let's now consider the coursework essay, 'An International Language', beginning with her paragraph by paragraph outline:

para. 1. Introduction. Background on early international languages in Europe: Latin, Spanish and French

para. 2. The 19th century. First attempt at an artificial international language: Schleyer's Volapuk

para. 3. The 19th century. Introduction to Dr Zamenhof's Esperanto

para. 4. What is Esperanto? Quote Guerard. Facts about the language: number of speakers, vocabulary, etc.

para. 5. The 20th century. Four other attempts at artificial international languages: Interlingua, New Interlingua, Ido, Novial

para. 6. The rise of English, competing with the artificial languages for international acceptance

para. 7. Basic English created by Ogden; Gowers and *Plain Words*

para. 8. The future: Esperanto or English?

para. 9. Conclusion. At the Cannes Film Festival films dubbed into English for worldwide distribution; street in Cannes named after Dr Zamenhof, founder of Esperanto. English as a true international language, but Esperanto, like the other artificial languages, has failed to catch on.

Example of the coursework essay

On the following pages we reproduce 'An International Language' as the student wrote it. To save space, the typing here is single-spaced, and the margins have been reduced.

CATHCART POLYTECHNIC

Department of Humanities

Linguistics I

AN INTERNATIONAL LANGUAGE

Constance Trescot

English I

Submitted to John Smith

10 January 1985

1

An International Language

There have been many hopes that the human race might achieve greater unity by having one common language to speak instead of the 2,000 or so now spoken. Before the 16th century, Latin was the dominant language of Europe. It crossed all boundaries, and it was an international tongue spoken by educated persons regardless of their national origins. In the 16th century, the rise to power of Spain brought the Spanish language into prominence, although Latin still ruled amongst church and state officials. With the French Revolution and the establishment of the French Empire under Napoleon, French seemed likely to be the supreme language in Europe during the 19th century.

By the late 19th century, however, two attempts had been made to create an international language which belonged not to one nation but to all nations. The first attempt was made by a German priest, S.M. Schleyer, who invented Volapuk, or 'World-speak'. In an effort to be fair, Schleyer combined features of some major national languages, English, French and German, as well as Latin. He first displayed this language in 1880, and although it aroused a good deal of interest, it failed to make much headway in an era of highly charged nationalism.

The second attempt, Esperanto, had more impact. Invented in 1887 by a Polish philologist, Dr L. Zamenhof, it was also based on the main European languages. For a time, it seemed that Esperanto was going to be a powerful force amongst languages, but after the initial enthusiasm which led to the founding of Esperanto societies, hopes for it faded.

As Guerard has observed, 'Esperanto strives to simplify language. It takes advantage of previous language habits, it limits grammatical categories and the variety of sounds.' Everything possible had been done to make Esperanto an easy language to learn and yet flexible to use. Its word-root vocabulary is

921, with a growth in its general vocabulary from 6,000 in 1887 to over 50,000 today. At the moment, Esperanto has over 1,000,000 speakers in 83 countries with 50 national associations, and 100 periodicals are published in this language. Yet, despite this considerable use and acceptance, Esperanto has failed to gain official recognition as one of the United Nations' Official Languages.

Four other attempts to create an international language have been made in the 20th century. Interlingua, invented by the Italian mathematician Giuseppe Peano in 1903, was based on classical Latin and included a Latin-derived scientific vocabulary to make it more adaptable for modern use. In the late 1940s, the principles of this language were revived as New Interlingua, but interest in it again declined. Ido, created by the Frenchman Louis de Beaufront in 1907, attempted to breathe new life into Esperanto. Although Ido attracted supporters in the years immediately after the First World War, interest in it subsided thereafter in favour of traditional Esperanto. Novial, constructed by the Danish linguist Otto Jespersen, was developed in 1928, but was little used except for some experimental purposes.

One of the principal reasons for the failure of these attempts to create an international language was the rise of English as a world tongue. So wide has been its penetration that efforts have been made to create a simplified English which would serve as an easy-to-use universal language. The best known of these efforts was made in 1932 by a British psychologist, Charles Ogden, who created Basic English.

Ogden pared down the English vocabulary presently exceeding 500,000 words to 850, comprising 100 terms for operations, 400 for general words, 200 for 'picture words' and descriptive words, 100 for general qualities, and 50 for opposite qualities. In addition to using these 850 'building blocks', Ogden simplified the grammar and regularized singular/plural constructions. Despite the appealing simplicity of this scheme, however,

Basic English has not had the popularity that Ogden had hoped for it. Its greatest influence has been, perhaps, on critics of English writing, who have long campaigned for a more simplified official style in government forms and local-authority publications. The Plain English Campaign, together with the work of Sir Ernest Gowers, *Plain Words,* is probably the most lasting recognition of Ogden's effort to popularize a Basic English language.

The future for an artificially created international language such as Esperanto does not look bright. On the other hand, English is fast becoming the second language in many countries of the world. It is also dominant in the scientific community, and is the language of computing and technology, as well as air-traffic control. Many developing nations have adopted it as an official second language because English is seen to be neutral in the midst of tribal, racial and cultural divisions in these nations.

It is ironic that Cannes, the French Riviera town where Dr Zamenhof, the founder of Esperanto, lived, and that has a street named after him, is the setting of an important film festival where most of the films shown in 1984 had English soundtracks or were to be dubbed into English. During the festival, producers and directors negotiated with translators and dubbers in an effort to make their films more international in their appeal, by using English as the language of all film dialogue. Dr Zamenhof had a vision of one language breaking down the frontiers and eroding the nationalistic differences in the world. He would probably be disappointed that Esperanto has not yet achieved this goal, but perhaps pleased that English has arrived as a worldwide second language in many countries, even if it has done little to solve the world's many political and cultural problems.

4

BIBLIOGRAPHY

Cutts, M. and C. Maher. *Writing Plain English*. Plain
    English Publishers, 1982.

Foster, B. *The Changing English Language*. Pelican,
    1971.

French, P. 'On the road to dull uniformity', *The
    Observer*, 20 May 1984.

Gowers, E. *Plain Words*. Penguin, 1982.

Guerard, A.L. *A Short History of the International
    Language Movement*. New York Press, 1934.

Palmer, F. *Grammar*. Pelican, 1974.

Quirk, R. *Linguistics and Your Language*. New York
    Press, 1964.

Comments and questions on the sample essay

1. Is the title 'An International Language' appropriate? Does the word 'language' refer to Esperanto or English?

2. Is the historical background in paragraph 1 too much? too little? necessary at all?

3. Are the figures presented in paragraph 4 confusing? Could this numerical information be better presented in a visual way, with a table? Would the essay have benefited from illustrations or linguistic maps?

4. The material in paragraph 5 is arranged in chronological order, except for the reference 'In the late 1940s . . .' after 1903. Is this reference justified in this place? Could it have been placed elsewhere in the paragraph?

5. Is the description of Ogden's creation of Basic English, in paragraph 7, sufficiently detailed to be understandable?

6. Does the author make a good case for her assertion that 'The future of Esperanto . . . does not look bright'?

7. Is the word 'ironic' correctly used in the final paragraph? What is the 'irony' involved?

8. Is the author's style clear and concise? Is there enough variety in her sentence structure? Does she explain all unfamiliar terms, such as the names of the artificial languages?

9. What method of organization of material does the author use?

10. The author uses only one brief quotation and does not footnote it. How does she acknowledge its source? Is one quotation enough in an essay such as this one?

11. Considering the fact that her bibliography contains seven titles, should more of the information she uses be footnoted?

12. Is the final paragraph a suitable conclusion to the essay, on the basis of what has preceded it?

Few good essays come straight from lecture notes; most are the result of additional reading, research and thinking. One of the reasons examiners set essays is to stimulate you into further reading in your topic. It is, therefore, essential to take notes from your reading, to analyse these notes, and to be critical in using them.

Plagiarism is theft.

Plagiarism

Plagiarism (from the Latin *plagiarius*, a kidnapper) is defined as the act of knowingly using another person's thoughts, writing or inventions as one's own.

We are all guilty of a certain amount of this kind of 'kidnapping' without knowing that we are. Much of our writing and thinking depends on other people's ideas and, to some extent, their words and phrases, which we seldom if ever credit to them. For instance, such expressions as 'pound of flesh' (Shakespeare), 'the best laid schemes o' mice an' men' (Robert Burns) and 'to err is human' (Alexander Pope) were originated from famous authors but we use them freely as part of the common currency of the language, rarely acknowledging the sources, although this use of the expressions is not regarded as plagiarism.

If, however, we deliberately copy passages from an author's work into our essays, without any acknowledgement of the source in a foot-note or inverted commas or in-text brackets with a reference to the work or bibliographic entry, that is a different kind of 'kidnapping' — it is stealing.

It is not an offence to use other people's ideas or to take material from others' books, or from newspapers, journals, or TV and radio pro-grammes, provided that you are not infringing copyright laws and that you also indicate clearly to the reader that you have borrowed the ideas or material in the form of adequate documentation.

Quality of expression

When essays are read for grading, the quality of expression used is also assessed. Whether the topic is English, or economics, or engineering, or chemistry, or computing, the reader is bound to be influenced by the way it is written in the essay, by the ease — or difficulty — with which the ideas and facts are communicated. If the quality of expression is to be considered good, the writing should be clear, correct, coherent and con-cise.

Use of English:
6 points to watch

The points you want to watch for in your own essays are:

1. good structure, each paragraph with a topic or summary sentence to guide the reader from idea to idea

2. variety in sentence structure, to avoid monotony for the reader

3. accurate spelling, so as not to confuse or irritate the reader

4. careful punctuation, to ensure clarity of meaning

5. relevance of information, in order to keep the reader's attention on the subject

6. topicality, to show the reader that you have studied the up-to-date examples and references

You will see from this list of points that everything is for the conveni-ence of the reader, nothing for the convenience of the author — you!

Revising and
proofreading

Before handing in an essay for grading, you should rewrite, or at least revise, the text from beginning to end, adding ideas or facts omitted from the first draft, deleting irrelevant or redundant material, checking your information for accuracy, and perfecting your style. It may also be help-ful to let a friend read over your essay with a view to making construc-tive critical comments on its content, form and style, and you yourself should scrupulously proofread every word and line of text to catch, and correct, errors and slips of the pen. If you take our advice seriously, you will find that your essays will be better pieces of writing, and the improvement will be reflected in better grades as well.

Student as teacher
in a good essay

Writing a good essay is not easy. It is a skill that takes much practice to acquire. The test of the success of any essay is in the reading of it, and if the reader, who is also assessing the essay, can understand it, and follow where you are leading him or her, then the reader's work becomes less of a chore, and more of a pleasure. Besides, the reader will probably become more open to your ideas and more prepared to accept and learn from them — and you, the student, become the teacher.

SUMMARY OF THE MAIN POINTS

- An essay is an informal prose composition, in which the author presents information and/or opinion.

- There are four steps to follow in preparing an essay:
  1. choice of topic
  2. construction of outline
  3. writing
  4. revision and proofreading

- The ingredients of a good essay are:
  1. relevance of material
  2. planning and organization of material
  3. clear, correct, concise and coherent style of writing
  4. neat, accessible layout

- Take time, take care, and take pride in preparing your written work. Good marks depend on these 'takes'!

Further Reading

Barrass, R.	*Scientists Must Write.* Chapman and Hall, 1979.
Barrass, R.	*Students Must Write.* Methuen, 1982.
Buzan, A.	*Use Your Head.* BBC Publications, 1974.
Martin, L. and H. Knoiter	*The 500-Word Theme.* Prentice-Hall (U.S.A.), 1979.
Rowse, S.	*Writing Essays in Social Science.* NEC, 1978.
Smithson, S.	*Business Communication Today.* ICSA Cambridge, 1983.

Chapter 12 The Report

What is a report?

A report (from the Latin *re,* back, and *porto,* carry) is a document which systematically and objectively presents specific information as accurately and as concisely as possible to a specific reader. Of varying length, but longer than a letter or a memo, a report usually falls into one of these four categories according to the terms of reference given in the assignment:

1. *informative:* to present statements of fact, with opinions, if called for, stated separately

2. *persuasive:* to obtain approval or agreement from your reader, or to recommend a certain course of action

3. *explanatory:* to answer questions and give conclusions

4. *historical:* to record an event or the results of an interview or a verbal agreement, or the evidence of work which has been done

Terms of reference

The report may be written on a business, social science, scientific or technical topic. The terms of reference are the specific instructions or limits (e.g., title or topic, length, date due, number of sources to be consulted, whether to include recommendations or not, and the like) given to you, the report writer. It is vital that you follow the instructions exactly or keep firmly within the limits set for you. Failure to do so will seriously diminish the effectiveness of your report.

Your reader

Your first duty as a researcher and writer is to your reader. You must take into account your reader's needs, attitudes, and knowledge of the topic of your report. These considerations will influence your choice of content as well as the kind of language you use. Ask yourself these questions:

- who is my reader?
- why does he or she want the report?
- what does he or she already know about the topic?
- what kind of language will he or she understand? (For example, too many technical or scientific terms may be inappropriate.)

Five points in the production of a report

The five points to consider in the production of a report are:

1. preparation
2. collecting material
3. organization of material
4. writing
5. revision

Preparation

Careful preparation is the basis of an effective report. First, establish clearly in your mind the topic and purpose of your report. Second, know what the terms of reference or the specific instructions are, and follow them to the letter. Third, know the date when the report is to be submitted, so that you will be sure to have enough time to produce the report properly. Fourth, keep your reader firmly in mind as you proceed to collect the material for your report and write it.

Collecting material

See also Chapter 8. Before you start collecting the material, check your terms of reference, review your purpose, and try to anticipate likely difficulties and obstacles that you might encounter.

You will collect material from a variety of sources and by a variety of methods. You will probably start by checking material already available in books, reference works, periodicals, and other kinds of publications. You may also want to conduct interviews with people who have information or expertise you need; visit places and sites; carry out experi-

'Carry out experiments and record the results.'

ments and record the results; and conduct surveys. In certain cases, you may want to draw upon your own personal knowledge or experience as a source of material to be used in your report.

Note taking

At this first stage, take down notes on everything which seems relevant, but check all facts and statements for accuracy. You may follow any order, unless the material obviously falls under the separate headings or into the natural divisions of your topic. If this is the case, keep separate sheets or notebooks for the recording of the different material.

Study and evaluate material

At the second stage, you will study the material you have collected, sorting through it and evaluating it according to the standards of your topic and to the terms of reference of your report. Not all facts, statements and ideas will be of equal value or relevance. You will want to verify facts, test statements, and weigh ideas for their soundness in the process of sifting through your material.

Reject/retain material

At the third and final stage of collecting material, you will reject certain items and retain only those which are required for your report. As you sort and sift your material:

1. reject all facts, statements and ideas which do not bear directly on your topic and particular purpose, no matter how interesting such material may be

2. retain only those provable facts, reliable statements, and sound ideas which your reader needs to know for his or her understanding of your topic

3. also retain those connecting items necessary for the coherent and complete presentation of your material

4. make sure that you have not omitted any facts, assumptions or propositions necessary to forming the logical conclusion to your report

Organization of material

See also Chapter 9. The next stage is to organize your material. How you organize it depends on the kind of topic you have researched, its purpose, scale and complexity. You may want to consider different methods of organization, such as logical, chronological, spatial, climactic/anticlimactic, or possibly some combination of these methods. In any case, your report will have the three basic organizational divisions:

1. introduction (beginning)

2. development (main text)

3. conclusion (end)

and should cohere in all its elements.

Steps to follow in organizing material

To help you organize your material, here are ten steps to follow:

1. write down your purpose in one sentence, which will test your grasp of your material.

2. choose a title (unless it is given) that makes your purpose clear

3. divide your main text, with its numbered headings, into lettered sub-headings, each of which will identify the subject matter under it

4. write each sub-heading on a separate sheet of paper and list your selected items in brief note form under the appropriate sub-headings

5. decide the order in which you will present the sub-headings, which will form the development (main text) of your report

6. arrange your material under each sub-heading in an order which your reader will be able to follow easily

7. consider what use you can make of illustrations, diagrams, maps, charts, tables, etc., to enhance your report

8. place tables of figures, lengthy calculations, extra-large maps and illustrations, glossaries, etc., in appendices to the report with references to them in the main text wherever relevant

9. decide where you want to present your conclusions and/or recommendations, either at the end of the whole report or the

end of each section, or both places, depending on the length and scope of the report itself

10. double check your conclusions and/or recommendations to ensure that they follow logically from and are consistent with the facts, statements and ideas presented in the main text

Writing your report

With all these steps in mind, you can now begin writing your report. (You will find a sample report at the end of this chapter, which illustrates many of the points below.) First, consider your style. It should be clear, concise, factual, and impersonal (that is, it should *not* include 'I', 'me', 'my', and 'mine' pronouns). The tone should be business-like, balanced and impartial.

Points about language

Here are some points to consider about your language in the report.

1. Prefer short, familiar, specific words to long, strange, abstract ones.

2. Be sparing in use of adverbs and adjectives.

3. Avoid jargon, slang and 'officialese'.

4. Avoid long-winded expressions.

5. Keep sentences short.

6. Explain terms the reader may not understand, in the text, in footnotes, or in a glossary (a mini-dictionary) at the end of your report.

Use of passive voice

In the grammar section, we noted that a verb has two voices, active and passive, e.g.:

active: I opened the door.

passive: The door was opened by me.

The effect of the passive voice is to reduce the emphasis on the personal pronoun (here 'I') as the doer of the action in a sentence. An even less personal statement might be achieved by changing this active voice sentence:

I recorded the fluctuations in pressure at hourly intervals . . .

to the passive voice:

The fluctuations in pressure were recorded at hourly intervals . . .

in which the doer, 'I', is eliminated altogether, and the emphasis falls on the recording of the fluctuations.

Objective style

College and university departments and business organizations generally prefer you to write your reports in the passive voice, which lends an objectively 'scientific' tone to your style.

Disadvantage: wordiness

One disadvantage of using the passive voice is that it is almost always wordier than the active:

active: The explosion injured the engineer.   (5 words)

passive: The engineer was injured by the explosion.   (7 words)

If you are writing a long report, all in the passive voice, the text will gain in wordage but not in substance.

Advantage: avoids tedious lists

On the other hand, where many indidivuals or teams were involved in a process or operation, it would be very tedious to name all the persons who contributed to the efforts, as in this example in the active voice:

Mr Jones, the engineer, helped make the unit function; Mrs Smith tested it; and Mr Brown put it into operation.   (20 words)

Here the passive voice is useful, and more concise:

The unit was produced by one of our engineers, then tested and put into operation by the department.   (18 words)

Mixing active and passive voices

It is possible of course, to rephrase this sentence in the active voice, producing a still more concise version:

One of our engineers produced the unit, which the department tested and put into operation.   (15 words)

This is not only more concise, but also stronger in effect than the passive-voice construction. In practice, you will be writing a mixture of sentences in both the active and passive voices. The active keeps your style forceful and direct, while the passive helps reduce the personal references, which may become tedious or be inappropriate when you are objectively discussing facts or procedures in a report.

Layout of report

Now let's consider the layout of the report. The presentation and appearance of your text should, as much as possible, reveal its structure. Pages and pages of unbroken text without sufficient headings and subheadings and no or only minimal margins will repel your reader. The 'eye appeal' of your report is important. In preparing the layout, you may be guided by the conventions established by the 'house style' of your department or institution. If you have no conventions to guide you in the layout, you may find the ones we give below to be useful. You may also wish to adapt them to your own needs. Examples of our conventions are given in the sample report presented later in this chapter.

Title page

The title page should contain all the information that any reader would need to know if he or she were to refer to your report as a source in a bibliography, namely:

- the name of the organization or institution where your report is prepared
- the name of the department for which the report is written
- the name of the course for which the report is written
- the title of your report, which briefly states the topic
- your name as author
- the name of your course and year

- the name of the lecturer or examiner or other person to whom the report is submitted
- the date of submission of the report

Margins

These items can be either centred or lined up on the left on the title page, but either way, the words and numerals should be neat, clear, and legible.

Margins of $1\frac{1}{2}''$ (4 cm) on every side of the text on all pages will serve as a frame for the text and help the reader to focus his or her attention on it. Margins also provide space where your reader can write comments, criticisms and corrections.

Contents page

To aid the reader, insert a contents page immediately after the title page. The contents page should consist of a list of all the items in the report, such as, the numbered headings, the lettered sub-headings, numbered figures (maps, charts, diagrams, etc.), bibliography, and appendix/appendices (if any). These items should be placed down the left-hand side of the page, with the relevant page numbers always down the right-hand side of the page. Begin numbering the pages with the first item in the report, the summary or abstract. In a short report, a detailed contents page will serve the same purpose as an index, which normally goes at the end of a report or book, and lists the contents in alphabetical order by subject headings, with page references.

Summary/abstract

To assist the reader gain a general view of the contents of the report, a short summary or abstract of the topic is placed next, just after the contents page and before the introduction, although it is sometimes placed at the end of the report as a kind of second conclusion. The summary or abstract may also include mention of keywords used in gaining access to computer-based information.

Introduction

This important section of your report should also be brief. In it, you should state your purpose (called terms of reference in some situations), name the particulars which you will deal with in the main text (development), and indicate what your conclusion is. You may also want to use the introduction to define a situation, theme, method or subject, and briefly indicate the extent and significance of the report. The introduction is important to you as well as to the reader, because it is the outline or blueprint of the whole report. By following it exactly, you will not stray beyond the declared purpose and particulars of your report.

Development (main text)

The development (or main text) section is the subject matter of your report, presented under a numbered main heading or headings which may give the title of your report. The main heading is followed by a series of lettered sub-headings identifying the sub-divisions of the topic. Under each of the sub-headings come numbered paragraphs in which the particular aspects (as noted in the introduction) are developed in a logical and coherent manner. Each sub-division should be of approximately the same importance. All the sub-divisions taken together must equal the topic being reported on as defined and particularized in the introduction.

Under the various lettered sub-headings you may need to:

- present facts, statements and ideas obtained through your research, and indicate their sources
- analyse or summarize these findings
- describe the procedures followed in your investigations, such as, experiments, questionnaires, surveys, and interviews
- refer to, or summarize, material fully presented in an appendix or the appendices
- state the conclusions or recommendations based on your findings (depending on the terms of reference)

Use of statistics and visuals

The use of statistics and/or visuals in your report can enhance its content and presentation. We offer you these suggestions:

- Include figures (maps, diagrams, charts, etc.) in the text only when they are necessary.
- Set out the figures by the text to which they refer.
- Visuals should be neatly mounted and bordered in ink to enhance their 'eye appeal'.
- Assign each visual a figure number (use the abbreviation 'Fig.' with the number in Arabic numerals) and identifying caption. This should be set *below* the visual.
- Explain any symbols you use.
- Explain the significance of any statistic you use.
- Round up figures in statistics and use units which the reader can remember (include the full numbers to several decimals in an appendix).
- Take care not to mislead the reader with distorted or exaggerated statistics.

Consistency

The consistency of the presentation and development of your material contributes to the success of your report. To ensure this consistency, do not:

- include irrelevant material
- present unfamiliar material without explanation
- omit essential steps in logical arguments
- elaborate the obvious
- present facts, statements or ideas in a random, unstructured way
- emphasize facts or ideas of secondary importance

Numbering and lettering

In using numbers and letters for the main headings, sub-headings and paragraphs of your report, it is necessary to be mindful of departmental or institutional practices and of your reader's needs. We recommend a choice of two styles:

THE EXPERIMENT, THAT IS THE TEST OR INVESTIGATION PLANNED TO PROVIDE EVIDENCE FOR OR AGAINST A HYPOTHESIS....!!

Do not elaborate the obvious.

1. capital Roman numerals (I, II, III, etc.) for main headings, capital Roman letters (A, B, C, etc.) for sub-headings, and Arabic numerals (1, 2, 3, etc.) for paragraphs, as in our sample report at the end of this chapter

2. modified decimal system (1.1, 1.2, 1.3; 2.1, 2.2, 2.3, etc.) used consecutively in numbering paragraphs

Whichever style you use, your numbering and lettering should be consistent throughout the report. Don't mix two styles in one report. Choose one and stick to it.

Page numbering

We suggest that you number the pages of your report in consecutive order starting with the summary or abstract page, and place the numbers in the upper right-hand corner of each page. Appendix pages should also be numbered. The two preliminary sections, the title and contents pages, are counted in the total number of pages, but not numbered.

Documentation

Another important feature of your report, which is written from researched material, is documentation, i.e., footnotes and bibliography. We advise you to ask whether your department or institution has a standard system of documentation or 'house style' which you are expected to use. If so, use it. If no system or 'style' is prescribed, you may find the following notes on documentation helpful.

Documentation is primarily a means of identifying sources and making references to those sources in the text of a piece of researched writing. There is more than one way to write footnotes and bibliographic entries, but the ways we suggest below are probably acceptable in most circumstances and for most purposes connected with report writing.

Footnotes

Footnotes are used in the main text for three general purposes:

1. to indicate the source of information or a quotation or both in your research material

2. to explain technical or unfamiliar terms, words or phrases, or foreign words

3. to add extra information that does not find a proper place in the main text

As the word 'footnote' indicates, it is a note which goes at the foot of the page of text, although in very long reports, containing many footnotes, these may be collected together on several pages at the end of the report. Keep the following points in mind when you write footnotes:

- Number them with Arabic numerals in consecutive order (1, 2, 3, etc.) throughout the report, including appendix pages. These numbers always go at the *end* of the word or passage being footnoted.

- Avoid using asterisks (*), daggers (†), crosses (+) and other such typographical symbols to indicate footnote references, because if you have a lot of footnotes, you will soon run out of symbols. You may occasionally use the asterisk in certain special circumstances, for example, to avoid confusion among references or to refer to words which are defined in a glossary placed elsewhere in the report.

- Don't start renumbering footnotes from 1 on each new page of the report — you will create confusion for the reader by having more than one footnote with the same reference number.

- Renumber your footnotes from 1 only when you begin a new chapter or major section in a long report, to avoid having many high-numbered footnotes.

- Keep footnotes on the same page as the reference numbers in the text.

- Draw a short line perhaps 1" (2.5 cm) long to separate the bottom line of the text from the footnote area, so that the reader does not confuse text and documentation.

- Keep footnotes brief, but if they must be long, perhaps they should be shifted to a page in an appendix.

The writing of footnotes is sometimes complicated by the use of certain Latin terms and abbreviations, but we suggest a simplified system using only English words. On the next page is a sample page with four footnotes. It is impossible to give examples of every type of footnote you may have to use, but these four will indicate the general style, which you can adapt to your needs.

```
┌─────────────────────────────────────────────────────┐
│ II. THE CONQUEST OF EVEREST                           │
│   A. The Setting: the Himalayas in Nepal              │
│     1. – – – – – – – – – – – – – – – – – – – – – – –   │
│     – – – – –, '.... quotation ....'¹                  │
│     2. – – – – – – – – – Sherpas² – – – – – – – – – –  │
│     – – – – – .                                        │
│     3. – – – – – – – – – – – – – – – – – – – – – – –    │
│     – – – – – – – – – – – – – ³                         │
│   B. Hillary's Preparations                            │
│     1. – – – – – – – – – – – – – – – – – – – – – – –     │
│     – – – – – .                                         │
│     2. – – – – – –, '.... quotation ...................  │
│     ..........'⁴                                         │
│     3. – – – – – – – – – – – – – – – – – – – – – – –      │
│     – – – – – – (see Appendix A).                        │
│   ─────────────                                          │
│   1  Fred Smith, Everest, p. 5.                          │
│   2  'Sherpas' are a Tibetan people living on the southern│
│   slopes of the Himalayas in Nepal, noted as mountaineers.│
│   3  All previous attempts to climb to the top of Mt Everest│
│   were unsuccessful.                                      │
│   4  Smith, p. 20.                                        │
└─────────────────────────────────────────────────────┘
```

In the sample page, observe the following points:

- Footnote 1 (notice that the reference number in the text is raised slightly above the line of writing, and comes at the *end* of the item being referred to) cites the source of a quotation from a book by Fred Smith, giving the page number.

- The next reference, footnote 4, to Smith's book will be simply the author's name and the new page number. Where there are authors with the same surname, give their first names, too, to distinguish them.

- Footnote 2 defines a foreign (and possibly unfamiliar) word.

- Footnote 3 adds some extra information on previous attempts to climb Mt Everest.

- The punctuation used is important, as it is part of the footnote and helps to convey its meaning.

- All the footnotes are contained within the writing area, leaving the 1½″ (4 cm) margin (not shown on sample page) intact.

- References to an appendix appear in the text, not as footnotes.

Bibliography

The bibliography is a list of sources and references used in researching your report topic. It is placed at the end of the report, immediately after the conclusion and/or recommendations. The basic information included in a bibliographic entry for a book and a magazine is as follows:

- book:
  1. author
  2. title of work
  3. facts of publication
     a. city of publication
     b. publishers' name
     c. date of publication
- magazine article
  1. author
  2. title of article,
     then title of magazine
  3. serial information:
     volume number, issue number
  4. date of publication
  5. inclusive pages of article

As with footnotes, there are different styles for writing bibliographic entries. We present below several examples of entries in a style which you are likely to find acceptable and useful in most circumstances and for most purposes, but you may have to adapt them to your own needs. If your department or institution has its own 'house style', you will, of course, use that instead.

BIBLIOGRAPHY

Magazine article	Adams, Bill. 'Climbing Everest', *Mountaineering Journal,* Vol. II, No. 5, May 1958, pp. 10-30.
Book with two authors	Brown, Edward and Sam White. *Sir Edmund Hillary.* London: Climbers' Press, 1980.
Interview	Carlyle, Thomas. Interview on Climbing Mount Everest. Glasgow: Interviewed by Paul Black, 20 March 1984.
Anonymous encyclopaedia article	'Himalayas', in *Encyclopaedia of Mountaineering,* John Smith, editor. London: Climbers' Press, 1964, Vol. II, pp. 50-60.
New edition of book with one author	Smith, Fred. *Everest,* 2nd ed. New York: Mountain Press, 1981.
Pamphlet with no facts of publication, or page numbers	Wilson, Jack. *Personal Experiences on Everest.* Pamphlet. No city: no publishers, no date. Unpaged.

In the foregoing examples, notice that:

- The entries are listed in alphabetical order by the author's last name or by title where no author is given. (When you have two or more works by the same author, list them in chronological order by date of publication.)

- Where there are two (or more) authors, only the first author's name (as given on the book's title page) is inverted for alphabetical listing.

- The second line in each entry is indented about half an inch (1.25 cm) so that the author's name or title stands out more prominently.

- Where the author is unknown, the entry begins with the title, as in the encyclopaedia article.

- An interview can be treated like any other source, with the person interviewed serving as author, subject of the interview as the title (but not underlined or put in inverted commas), place of interview as city of publication, interviewer as the person who makes the interview public (or 'publisher'), and date of interview as 'date of publication'.

- Some documents provide incomplete information, in which case you describe the work as accurately as possible in your own words, as in the case of the pamphlet.

- It is not necessary to note inclusive page numbers for a book, only for magazine or encyclopaedia articles.

In a short bibliography, it is not necessary to number the entries. Only in a very long bibliography would it be useful to do so. Nor is there any need to sub-divide the entries into separate sections for books, magazine articles, etc., unless your bibliography is a very long one and the sub-divisions would serve a practical purpose for the reader. Generally, the necessary bibliographic data for a book can be obtained from the title page and the reverse side, called the copyright or imprint page.

Bibliography for the reader

The bibliography is a record of your sources presented for the reader's information, use and convenience. The information in the bibliographic entries should be as complete and accurate as possible (but you cannot give information that is not in the source itself) so that the reader can easily trace your sources to consult them if he or she wishes to do so.

Conclusion

The conclusion of your report should stem directly from and summarize the facts, statements, ideas and other findings presented in the development (main text). Extraneous observations and purely personal opinions should be excluded. The length of the conclusion will vary from report to report, depending on the kind and scope of the topic, but generally the conclusion should be short and to the point.

Recommendations

Not all reports contain sections devoted to recommendations. If they are needed, they will probably be observations of an advisory nature which require action to be taken. They should be practicable. Sometimes careful tabulation of data helps in presenting recommendations. They may refer to any wider consideration outside your terms of reference on which your report may have a bearing. They, too, should be short and to the point. They will probably be written as a section separate from and following the conclusion.

Appendix/appendices

The appendix (if the report includes one at all) will probably consist of extensive calculations, statistics, large diagrams, and other supplementary or substantiating material. These items should also be footnoted if they are borrowed from research sources, but not if they are original to you. If there is more than one appendix, they should be lettered (A, B, C, etc.) or numbered (I, II, III, etc.) in consecutive order (but don't mix letters and numbers), and placed as the final section of your report, after the bibliography, which follows the conclusion and (if you have them) the recommendations.

Revision

We advise you to write your report in at least two drafts. The first draft will be rather rough, requiring correction, rewriting and polishing. The second, corrected draft will be prepared in a fair copy, preferably typed, to be handed in for assessment. Remember to keep a copy (photocopy or carbon) of your report for your own files.

Before preparing your second draft, put the report aside for a day or two, if time permits. Then read it over objectively and critically, as if it were another student's work, and consider these points and questions:

- Look at the report as a whole. Is the design clear? Are the headings and sub-headings consistent with your purpose?

- Examine the title page, contents page, summary, introduction, and conclusion/recommendations in relation to one another. Are they consistent with one another? Have you stated your purpose and particulars clearly in the introduction?

- Weigh every statement in the main text for accuracy, relevance and coherence.

- Check the spelling, punctuation and grammar in your writing.

- Check your illustrations, diagrams, charts, tables, maps, etc., to ensure that they contribute to the purpose and content of the report. Are all the visuals properly identified, with figure numbers and captions?

- Look over the layout, checking on spacing, margins, page numbers, and general neatness.

- Check on the accuracy and style of your footnotes and bibliography.

If you are satisfied with the final draft, you may want to enclose it in a protective folder before handing it in for assessment.

Sample report by David Dewar

The sample report presented on the following pages was written by a first-year student, Mr David Dewar, in the Department of Electrical and Electronic Engineering, Paisley College of Technology, for a course in Communication, on a topic he chose himself, 'How an Electronic Music Synthesizer Works'. He received very specific instructions for this assignment, which were:

1. Total counted wordage: 1140, including:

    a. summary (or abstract): 40 words

    b. introduction: 50 words (to be written as one sentence)

    c. main text: 1000 words

    d. conclusion: 50 words (to be written as one sentence)

    - No recommendations were required, and appendix/appendices were optional

2. Uncounted wordage included:

    a. title page

    b. contents page

    c. all headings and sub-headings

    d. all quotations

    e. all figure numbers and captions

    f. all footnotes

    g. bibliography

    h. appendix/appendices

3. Required components of the report included:

    a. minimum of three different research sources, written in prescribed style, as above

    b. minimum of six footnotes, written in prescribed style, as above, and numbered in consecutive order

    c. minimum of four quotations to support topic

d. minimum of five illustrations, diagrams or other kinds of supplementary material, including material in an appendix

e. margins of 1½″ (4 cm) all round on each page

f. pages numbered from summary page, in consecutive order throughout the report, marked in upper right-hand corner

Sample report can be adapted

The layout, structure and documentation styles shown in the sample report may be adapted to your own needs, rather than slavishly copied. The report is meant to be helpful to you if you have no other guide to follow. Different departments and institutions and lecturers have different ideas and practices, so you must be flexible in approaching report writing. But whatever the techniques and styles you use, remember that everything you write is for the convenience of the reader, to make it easy for him or her to understand what you have to report.

The sample report starts on the next page. To save space, the typing is here single-spaced, and the margins have been reduced.

Keep your reader interested.

PAISLEY COLLEGE OF TECHNOLOGY

Department of Social Studies

Communication

HOW AN ELECTRONIC MUSIC SYNTHESIZER WORKS

David Dewar

E.E.E. I E2

Submitted to Konrad Hopkins

23 March 1984

CONTENTS

1

SUMMARY (or ABSTRACT)
This report concerns how an electronic music
synthesizer works, concluding that it can be
described by considering distinct sections of the
instrument one by one.

Keywords: electronic music synthesizer
                oscillator
                control voltage source
                noise generator
                timbre control
                amplitude control

2

I. INTRODUCTION

The purpose of this report is to describe how an
electronic music synthesizer works, in particular,
oscillators, control voltage sources, noise generators,
timbre control and amplitude control, showing that
although a synthesizer is a complex piece of
equipment, it can be easily broken down into much
simpler building blocks.

II. HOW AN ELECTRONIC MUSIC SYNTHESIZER WORKS

A. Definition

1. A synthesizer can best be defined as 'a device that constructs a sound by determining uniquely the fundamental elements of pitch*, timbre* and loudness*'[1] (for all terms marked with * see Appendix A). These fundamental elements that describe a sound are controlled by different parts of the synthesizer. First, the <u>oscillator</u> creates the original signal. Then it is processed by a <u>filter</u>, which adjusts the tonal quality. Lastly, the filtered signal is processed by an <u>amplifier</u>, which controls the lever or loudness of the final sound.

B. Oscillators

1. 'The oscillator is the starting point for the generation of a sound. It is required to produce an output with a fixed harmonic content and a fixed level but with complete control over the frequency.'[2] The signal or waveform produced is 'an alternating voltage* of a few volts with a frequency which can be varied over the audio range*'.[3] The level of the signal determines its amplitude (loudness) and the harmonic content determines its tonal quality (timbre). These properties are further modified by parts of the synthesizer yet to be discussed.

2. Different waveforms are selected by a switch on the front panel. The three main waveforms used are known as squarewave, sawtooth and triangle (see Fig. 1).

3. These are eventually heard as pitched tones, whose pitch depends on the number of times one cycle repeats in one second. This is the frequency.

---

1 D. Crombie, *The Complete Synthesizer*, p. 7.
2 M.K. Berry, *Electronic Music and Creative Tape Recording*, p. 19.
3 J. Jenkins *et al.*, *Electric Music*, p. 24.

4

1. Squarewave

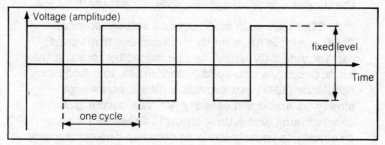

2. Sawtooth

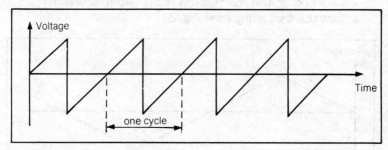

3. Triangle

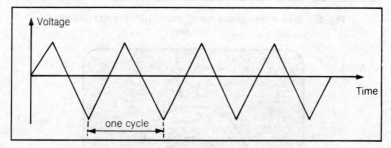

Fig. 1   Three main oscillator output waveforms

C. Control Voltage Sources

1. A control Voltage (CV) is a variable voltage*
which is applied to one or more parts of the
synthesizer to control certain parameters. The
oscillator frequency (pitch) is a voltage-controlled
parameter. Increasing the CV increases the
frequency. The oscillator is thus called a voltage-
controlled oscillator (VCO). Other devices may also be
voltage-controlled. 'A voltage-controlled instrument
has one or more operating parameters determined by

5

the magnitude of an applied control voltage.'[4]

2. There are four main control voltage sources. First, a simple knob on the instrument front panel can provide a CV which can be varied by rotating the knob. Second, a non-voltage-controlled, low-frequency oscillator (LFO) can provide a CV which sweeps slowly up and down (see Fig. 2). The output is a slowly rising and falling triangle waveform whose frequency is usually variable between one cycle every ten seconds and about two cycles per second (see Fig. 2). A knob on the instrument front panel is used to adjust the frequency (see Fig. 3).

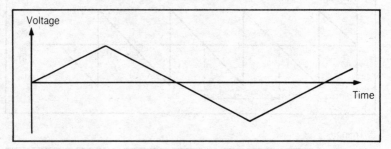

Fig. 2   A low-frequency oscillator (LFO) control-voltage source

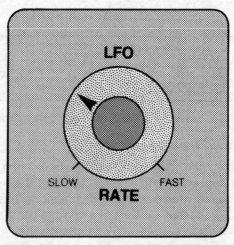

Fig. 3   Knob on the instrument front panel

4 Jenkins, p. 25.

6

3. The third CV source is essential, 'a keyboard provided with electrical contacts (beneath the keys) which provide different output voltages for each key pressed'.[5] This is required to control the VCO frequency, thus relating the pitch of the final sound to the key being depressed (see Fig. 4).

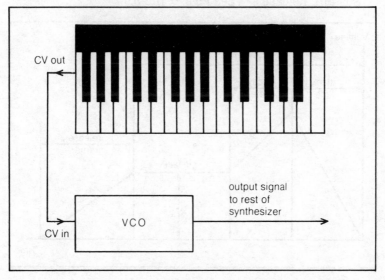

Fig. 4   Control of VCO pitch using the keyboard control voltage

4. The fourth CV source is a device called the envelope generator (EG) whose purpose will become apparent in the sections on timbre control (E) and amplitude control (F). Each note has what is known as an envelope. The loudness or timbre of the sound follows a contour or envelope shape. When a note is played, the envelope generator produces a control voltage which follows the desired contour. Unusual effects can be obtained by allowing the envelope to vary other voltage-controlled parameters, such as the pitch of the note.

5. Each time a key is pressed the EG produces its voltage contour as follows. 'When the key is closed and held down the envelope commences on its attack.

---

5 Berry, p. 24.

THE REPORT

It reaches a peak and immediately begins decaying away, but does not drop to zero. Instead it falls to a level that has been preset by the sustain control and stays there until the key is released when the envelope decays to zero at a rate set by the release control. This is the ADSR envelope (Attack, Decay, Sustain, Release).'[6] (See Figs. 5 and 6.)

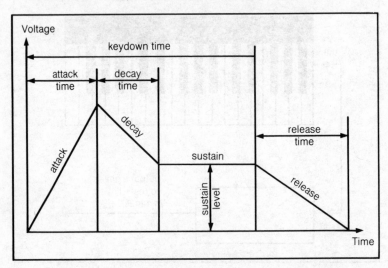

Fig. 5   The ADSR envelope generator (EG) control-voltage
contour

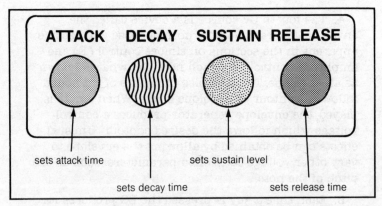

Fig. 6   Front panel controls for setting parameters

6 Berry, p. 29.

8

D. Noise Generators

1. The noise generator produces a waveform with randomly varying frequency and amplitude. This sounds like a radio which is not tuned in properly or the way *sh* sounds in a word like 'should'. There is no particular pitch associated with noise as it is made up of frequencies which vary randomly over the whole audio spectrum* (see Fig. 7).

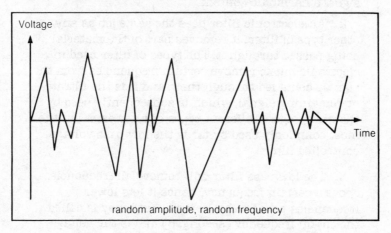

random amplitude, random frequency

Fig. 7 The noise generator output waveform

2. 'There are two main types of noise that are encountered when dealing with electronic music. First, white noise, which has an equal spread of frequencies right across the spectrum.'[7] This has the hissing quality described above (paragraph 1). 'The second is known as pink noise and is somewhat softer sounding, as it tends to be biased towards the frequencies at the lower end of the spectrum.'[8]

3. The noise generator is not voltage-controlled. It is represented on the instrument front panel by a switch to select pink or white noise and a knob to control how much of the output signal is taken to the rest of the synthesizer. To produce wind, thunder or surf sounds, the noise signal is modified by the timbre and amplitude control devices.

---

7 Crombie, p. 29.
8 Crombie, p. 29.

E. Timbre Control

1. The timbre of a sound is its tonal quality which is determined by its harmonic content*. All the waveforms produced by the VCO are rich in their respective harmonic contents. The timbre is controlled by passing the VCO output signal through an electronic filter which can remove part of the signal's harmonic content.

2. 'An electronic filter does the same job as any other type of filter: it removes part of the material being passed through it. The types of filter used in electronic music remove certain frequencies from the signals being fed through them and it is the filtrate, or remaining signal, which is subsequently used by the next stage.'[9] Different types of filter exist but the most commonly used by far is the low pass voltage controlled filter.

3. 'The low pass filter will remove all frequencies above a certain frequency, hence it lets lower frequencies pass.'[10] This certain frequency is called the cut-off frequency (see Fig. 8) and is the voltage-controlled parameter, hence the term voltage-controlled filter (VCF).

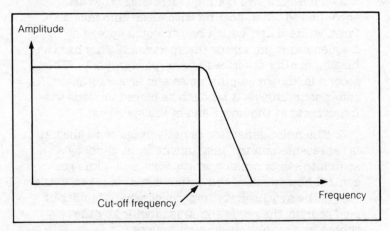

Fig. 8   The low-pass filter frequency response (output characteristic)

---

9 Crombie, p. 31.
10 Crombie, p. 31.

4. The cut-off frequency can be set by a knob on the front panel, or swept up and down by the low-frequency oscillator (LFO). Cut-off frequency can also be swept by an envelope generator each time a note is played.

F. Amplitude Control

1. When a note is played on an instrument the loudness or amplitude builds up to a peak and then decays away. This forms the amplitude envelope associated with the sound of that instrument (see Fig. 9).

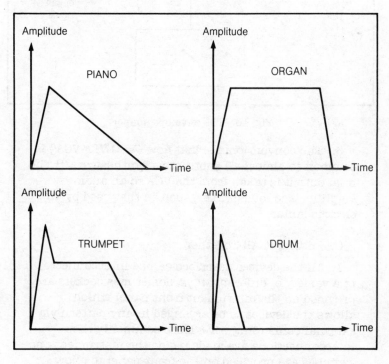

Fig. 9   Some examples of the amplitude envelopes for some well-known instruments

2. After passing through the filter, the signal is now passed through a voltage-controlled amplifier (VCA). The voltage-controlled amplifier controls the amplitude or loudness of the signal. The greater the

11

control voltage, the louder the sound. Usually, the
control voltage is taken from an envelope generator.
In this context, the envelope generator and VCA are
known collectively as the envelope shaper (see Fig.
10). This allows any envelope to be imparted on the
synthesizer output for each note played.

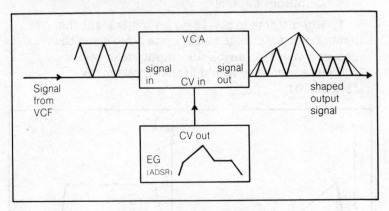

Fig. 10   The envelope shaper

3. 'The conventional signal flow (VCO-VCF-VCA) is
common to almost all subtractive synthesizers.'[11] The
final output is taken from the VCA to an audio
amplifier and loudspeaker, such as that used by an
electric guitar.

G. Putting It All Together

1. All the devices described can be interconnected
in a variety of different ways. Sometimes sockets are
provided on the instrument front panel which
allows the devices to be arranged in any pattern via
external connecting wire. More commonly the
interconnections are made inside the instrument and
switches are provided on the front panel to allow
limited variation in the patch*. The most common
patch is shown in Fig. 11.

11 Crombie, p. 55.

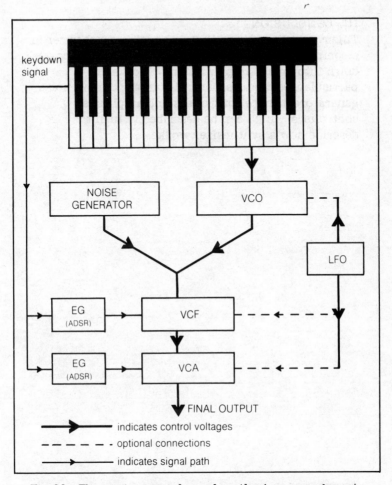

Fig. 11   The most commonly used synthesizer arrangement

13

III. CONCLUSION
This report has shown that although a synthesizer is
a complex piece of equipment, it can be easily broken
down into much simpler building blocks, in
particular, oscillators, control-voltage sources, noise
generators, timbre controllers and amplitude
controllers, which can be described in turn to
describe how a synthesizer works.

14

BIBLIOGRAPHY
Berry, M.K. *Electronic Music and Creative Tape
    Recording.* London: Bernard Babani, 1978.
Crombie, D. *The Complete Synthesizer.* London:
    Omnibus Press, 1982.
Jenkins, J. *et al. Electric Music.* Vancouver:
    Douglas, David and Charles Limited, 1975.

APPENDIX A

Glossary

Amplitude: In electronic music, amplitude means the magnitude of a signal or sound loudness.

Audio range/spectrum: There is a limit to the range of frequencies which can be detected by the human ear. The lower threshold is generally between 18 and 25 Hz. The ear can detect frequencies up to about 20,000 Hz. The range of human hearing is called the audio range or spectrum.

Frequency: The frequency of a signal or sound is the musical pitch and is measured by the number of cycles of the wave occurring in one second. (1 cycle/sec = 1 Hertz [Hz].)

Harmonics/harmonic content: A sound or signal consists of a fundamental frequency and a series of related harmonics which are multiples of the fundamental frequency. If the fundamental has the value f, then the first harmonic will have value 2f, the second 3f, etc. These are pitched at one, two, etc. octaves above the fundamental. Harmonic content is dependent on the wave shape.

Loudness: This is the volume of a sound or its audible intensity and is directly related to the amplitude of a signal from which the sound is derived.

Patch: This is the pattern of arrangement of the interconnected devices in the synthesizer.

Pitch: This is the musical term for frequency. Notes higher up the musical scale have higher pitch and hence higher frequency (see frequency).

16

Timbre: This is a musical term for tone, tonal
            quality, tone colour or sound texture. It is
            dependent on the harmonic content of a
            signal or subsequent sound wave.

Voltage: This is an electrical quantity measurable
            in volts. It can be transferred via wires
            from one part of the synthesizer to
            another. An alternating voltage
            continually changes between two values
            at regular time intervals. The way it does
            this describes a waveform.

17

APPENDIX B
Abbreviations
ADSR: attack, decay, sustain, release
CV: control voltage
EG: envelope generator
LFO: low-frequency oscillator
VCA: voltage-controlled amplifier
VCF: voltage-controlled filter
VCO: voltage-controlled oscillator

Comments and questions on the sample report

1. This is an informative/descriptive report, and the author uses the analytical method of presenting his material, which leads to a synthesis in the section 'G. Putting It All Together'. Is this the most effective method to use?

2. The author uses the minimum three sources for his information, as listed in his bibliography. Are these enough for his purpose in a technical, 1,000-word report?

3. The author uses eleven quotations (about 161 words altogether) in his text. How are they presented? Could any of them have been separated from the text and presented as single-spaced quotations for easier reading? Are there too many of them?

4. Is this technical topic written for easy understanding by a reader with no special knowledge of music synthesizers? Is the style appropriate to the topic? How does he use the active/passive voice?

5. Notice that the author uses the possessive personal pronoun 'whose' in a special connection, namely, in 'whose pitch', 'whose frequency', and 'whose purpose'. Is the usage acceptable in each instance? How could these phrases be worded differently to avoid using 'whose'?

6. Has the author used the words 'via', 'hence', 'etc.', and *'et al.'* (in footnote 4) correctly?

7. The diagrams are original with the author, and so do not need to be documented with footnotes. Do the diagrams help to explain the text? Are there enough of them or too many? Are they adequately captioned?

8. Notice the author's special use of the asterisk (*) to identify technical terms which he defines in Appendix A (as is noted in brackets in the text). Are these terms clearly defined?

9. Notice that Appendix A is a glossary (a word list) arranged in alphabetical order for reference. Is this the most useful way to order the information?

10. Appendix B is a list of abbreviations used and explained in the text. Is this list necessary?

11. The author's conclusion is a summary restatement of the contents of the main text, similar in wording to the introduction. Is this sufficient for a report of this kind? If not, what else might he have said?

SUMMARY OF THE MAIN POINTS

- Report layout may be governed by departmental or institutional 'house styles'.

- The five main points in the production of a report are:
  1. preparation
  2. collecting material
  3. organizing material
  4. writing
  5. revision/proofreading

- A report has three main organizational divisions:
  1. introduction/terms of reference
  2. development (main text)
  3. conclusion/recommendations

- Footnotes and bibliography (documentation) support the text with references to sources, while maps, charts, diagrams, tables, and other 'visuals' supplement the content of a report.

- Take time, take care, and take pride in preparing your written work. Good marks depend on these 'takes'!

Further Reading

Cooper, B.M.   *Writing Technical Reports.*
                Pelican, 1969.

Little, P.   *Communication in Business,*
                3rd ed. Longmans, 1977.

Turk, C. and   *Effective Writing.*
J. Kirkman.   E. & F.N. Spoon, 1982.

Chapter 13 Letters, C.V.'s, Application Forms

LETTERS

Two advantages to letters

There are two advantages that a letter has over a telephone call or a face-to-face conversation. One is that in a letter, the words have a certain permanence, and these are increasingly being stored in word-processor files. The other is that in a letter, the writer can clarify ideas and elaborate information accurately.

A major disadvantage

A major disadvantage of a letter is that if you make an error in the text and the letter is sent, there is almost no chance of retrieving it, whereas

the error you make in conversation can be quickly corrected. A faulty letter will probably require a follow-up message to correct the mistake.

Three types of letters

The three main types of letters are personal, official, and business. In this chapter, we will consider only those kinds of business letters which you are most likely to write, such as a letter:

- requesting an application form and further details
- requesting further information
- accepting a job offer
- applying for a job, with personal particulars
- accompanying an application form and C.V.
- requesting help in a research project

Points to bear in mind

Regardless of the type of letter you write, bear in mind that your letter:

- represents you and, to some extent, expresses your personality

- should be written in a style appropriate both to the person to whom the letter is addressed and to the purpose of the letter
- should have a neat, clean appearance, free of mistakes in spelling, punctuation, grammar, facts and figures
- should have a structure (logical and/or chronological) to help the reader understand your message

Ask yourself questions

To help you keep these principles in mind, put yourself in the readers position, and ask yourself these questions:

- How will this letter impress the reader?
- Are the style and tone right for the reader and the purpose of the letter?
- Is all the information that the reader will want included in the letter?
- Are all the facts and figures correct?
- Is the English clear?

Nine elements in business letters

We can identify nine elements which are usually found in business letters:

1. address of the sender
2. date of composition of the letter
3. direction
4. salutation
5. reference or heading
6. body of the letter
7. subscription
8. signature
9. postscript

Address, date, direction

For the position and layout of your address, the date and the direction (that is, the name and address of the person or company to whom you are writing), see the section on conventional layouts later in this chapter.

Salutation

The salutation, namely 'Dear', is the convention you follow in beginning a letter. If you know the name of the person to whom you are writing, you should begin, for example, 'Dear Mr Jones', 'Dear Ms Smith', etc. If you do not know to whom you are writing, you should begin, 'Dear Sir', 'Dear Sirs', 'Dear Sir/Madam', etc. Other forms may also be used, for example, in a circular letter, 'Dear Colleague', 'Dear Member', etc.

Reference or heading

It is customary to include the reference number of the letter to which you are replying, if there is such a reference number, or to place a subject heading above the body of the letter, if there is only one subject of the letter.

The subject heading is widely used nowadays. At a glance the reader can see what the letter is about, although it can also make the letter seem cold and over-formal, when perhaps a warmer and less rigid tone and form are needed. Use your own discretion in this matter. Here is an example of the subject heading in a letter:

Dear Member

<u>Golf Competition 1985</u>

I am writing to all members to ask whether they would help in the organization of this year's Grand Competition . . .

Use of 'Re'

'Re', meaning 'with reference to', is derived from the Latin *re,* dative case of *res,* thing. The word, in contexts such as 're your letter . . .' or 'he spoke to me re your complaint', is common in business or official correspondence. In general English, 'with reference to' is preferable in the former case, and 'about' or 'concerning' in the latter. The use of 're' is often restricted to the letter heading, but even there it is generally unnecessary.

Body of the letter

The text of your letter, unless very short, should be set out in several paragraphs, thus giving it an attractive appearance and making it more readable. If your letter concerns several different subjects, each one should be dealt with in a separate paragraph. Short, concise paragraphs may be more effective and impressive than long, involved constructions in which the reader may lose his or her way — and patience.

Arrange your points in some recognizable order, e.g., logical or chronological, to give your text a structure. Don't ramble; get to the point. Provide a summary of the main facts, which should be put in a definite sequence.

In laying out the text, leave a margin of 1″ or 1½″ (2.5 or 4 cm) all round to help focus the reader's attention on your message and to facilitate filing.

The introductory paragraph (or reference) reminds the reader of any previous correspondence, or refers to the purpose of the present letter, or mentions the advertisement that has prompted the letter.

The development (or body) of the letter presents such particulars as are needed to support the purpose of your letter.

The ending (or conclusion) of your letter states what you hope to receive in reply from the reader.

Example: letter requesting application form and further details

Here is an example of a letter requesting an application form and further details, illustrating the three main parts of the text:

Dear Sir/Madam

Introduction (Reference)

I refer to your advertisement in the <u>Cathcart Times</u> of Tuesday, March 5, 1985, for recruits to join 'Holiday Camp USA'.

Development (Body)

I am 22 years old and have considerable experience in organizing camping expeditions with the Scouts. I am, in fact, a Senior Scout, and have passed my first aid certificate with St John's Brigade.

I am in excellent health, and at present am studying at Cathcart Polytechnic (B.Sc. Eng.). I am very keen to travel to the USA and fully understand the responsibilities in connection with this undertaking.

Ending (Conclusion)

I would be grateful if you would send me an application form and further details.

Yours faithfully

J.P. McEager

Style

The style used in letters has changed greatly over the past twenty-five years. Generally, it has become less formal, more conversational. A plain, unaffected, natural style is best. Avoid flowery language, and artificial, pompous or antiquated expressions, such as:

I beg to reply . . .

I beg to thank you for . . .

Your esteemed favour to hand . . .

Your most humble and obedient servant . . .

Dates

When referring to dates in your letter, avoid these clumsy and outmoded forms

Your letter of the 6th *inst.*
                  (present month)

Your letter of the 20th *ult.*
                  (last month)

Our appointment of the 10th *prox.*
                  (next month)

Just write the date in the normal way, with the day and month. Mention the year only if it is not the current one.

Writing dates in the U.S.A. and U.K.

If you have occasion to receive or reply to letters sent from the U.S.A., remember that the American way of writing a date is different from that used in the U.K. For example:

U.S.A.: month/day/year: 4/11/85

U.K.: day/month/year: 11/4/85

Appropriate language

Considering the style of your letter, you must find the level of language appropriate to your reader and to the purpose of the letter. In most cases, you will want to avoid using jargon, the technical or special language peculiar to a particular profession or group, unless you are certain that the reader will understand it. Otherwise, the reader might be confused or put off or bewildered by words or phrases that he or she does not comprehend.

Tone

Another consideration in letter writing is tone, that is, the 'voice' or 'sound' of your words and the attitude which they project to the reader. Finding exactly the right tone is perhaps the most difficult task you have in composing a letter. Generally speaking, you can't go far wrong in your tone if you always express yourself courteously, even when you are writing a letter of complaint or criticism.

Subscription

Subscription means 'written under the text' and is also known as the closing phrase. Use 'Yours faithfully' when you don't know the name of the person to whom you are addressing the letter. When you do know the person's name, it is more friendly to use the subscription 'Yours sincerely'.

Signature

In most business letters, your initials and surname will be sufficient. Women may want to indicate their sex or marital status by adding 'Miss', 'Ms', or 'Mrs'. Print or type your name under your signature, so that there is no doubt as to what your name is.

Postscript

Postscript is from the Latin *postscriptum*, meaning something 'written after' the rest of the letter, and is indicated with 'P.S.' or just 'PS'. If the PS is needed, it should be kept short, and used only when there is really something extra to be added to the text, such as new information which has just come to hand.

Conventional layouts

There are two conventional layouts for letters: semi-blocked and blocked. Examples of each type of layout are shown in Figs. 1 and 2 on the following pages; each example has a numbered key identifying salient points.

Letters applying for a job

The letter of application for a job is perhaps the hardest of all the types of letters to write. Here are some points to consider:

- Plan your letter carefully.
- Draft it once, including all the relevant facts you can think of.
- Make the necessary corrections in the first draft, and prepare a second draft.
- Check that you have included all the essential details.
- Check that the details coincide with information requested in the advertisement.

(1) 5 Hartford Avenue,
BILSBERRY,
Berks.
BB6 7AZ

(3) Your ref:

(2) 10 April 1984

(4) The Training Officer,
(5) Dodo Publications plc.,
Row Lane,
HUDDERSFIELD,
Yorks,
HD3 2AB

Dear Training Officer,

   (6) I would be grateful if you could send me further information concerning the post of Assistant Training Officer, which was advertised in the Bilsberry Telegraph of 8 April 1984.

                    (7) Yours faithfully,

                      F.G. Earnmore

Key:

(1) The sender's name is written or typed in the top right-hand corner. The postal code is clearly identified. The sender's name is *not* included.

(2) The date appears beneath the sender's address and is aligned with it.

(3) If you have a reference number, it goes at the left-hand margin opposite the sender's address.

(4) The person to whom the letter is being written is identified by his or her official title.

(5) The recipient's address is not indented, and the postal code is included.

(6) The opening paragraph of the letter is indented.

(7) The formal closing phrase is used because the recipient's name is not given in the salutation.

Fig. 1   Example of semi-blocked layout

(1) DODO PUBLICATIONS plc
Row Lane, HUDDERSFIELD, YORKS
HD3 2AB   Tel. HUD 35431

(2) Our ref
Your ref

10 April 1984

Mr R Jones
Training Officer
(3) Camel Publications plc
ASHLEY
Herts
HT5 3AZ

Dear Mr Jones

Thank you for your letter of 1 April 1984 enclosing
plans for a training course in computer graphics for
staff involved in publishing.

We have given the course our serious consideration and
we would like to send five of our staff. Their names and
designations are enclosed.

We would like to thank you for all the hard work you
have put into setting up this course. We are sure that it
will be a great success.

Yours sincerely

M.M. Applecore

Key:
(1) The letter is usually typed on headed stationery.
(2) The typing begins at the left-hand margin.
(3) No punctuation is used except in the body of the letter.

Fig. 2   Example of blocked layout

- Write or type the letter clearly and neatly according to accepted layout.
- Check the letter for mistakes and make necessary corrections.
- Keep a copy of the letter for your files.
- Enclose an s.a.e. (stamped addressed envelope) if you expect a reply.
- Address the envelope as stated in the advertisement.

What to include

When you write the letter applying for a job, these are the basic facts about yourself to include:

- your full name
- your full address
- your age, birthday, nationality
- your marital status
- the post for which you are applying
- your education, work experience, training, special abilities or interests, etc., if no C.V. or application form is enclosed

Tone and style

Just as important as these facts are the qualities of politeness and frankness in your letter's tone, and the excellence of its style. Your writing should be correct in spelling, punctuation and grammar, and should avoid all expressions of flattery or servility, if you hope to make a favourable impression on the prospective employer.

Example: letter accompanying application form and C.V.

A covering letter to accompany your application form and your C.V. should be short and to the point, as in this example:

90 Lucky Drive,
GREYSLEY,
Strathclyde
GR1 5EY

25 January 1985

Personnel Officer
Blake, Blank and Black plc.
FOLDEROL
Foldshire
FO9 4OL

Dear Personnel Officer

<u>Post of Assistant Manager</u>

Enclosed for your consideration are my completed application form for the above post, as advertised in the <u>Cathcart Times</u> of 23 January 1985, and my curriculum vitae.

Yours faithfully

A.L. Hope

Example: letter of application without C.V. or application form

Here is an example of a letter of application for a job, without a curriculum vitae (C.V.) or application form enclosed.

> 10 Balwood Terrace
> GREYSLEY
> Strathclyde
> GR1 2EY

20 May 1985

The Training Officer
Stows Engineering plc.
STOWBRIDGE
Stowshire
ST5 2BR

Dear Training Officer

Post of Trainee Manager

I would like to apply for the above post as advertised in the Evening Mail of 30 April 1985.

My name is John Charles McNab. I am 20 years of age, born on 4 July 1965, and a British citizen. I am unmarried.

I am in my final year at Cathcart Polytechnic, and will take my Finals this June. My degree course is in Chemistry, and I have also taken Mathematics as a subsidiary subject.

During the degree course, I have worked in two summer vacations with J & R Strong, Engineering Works, Stowbridge. My duties involved assisting the Chief Chemist, reporting to him any problems with the plant and recording remedial action taken.

Although I enjoy the scientific side of chemical engineering, I have long had management as my chief career aim. This last year at Cathcart Polytechnic I chose an introductory course in Management run in conjunction with the Stowshire Junior Chamber of Commerce and Cathcart Polytechnic.

I am available for an interview at any time convenient to you.

Yours faithfully

J.C. McNab

Letters requesting help in a research project

In connection with a research project, you may find it necessary sometimes to write to organizations requesting specific information.

State precisely and concretely what information you want and why you want it. It helps, too, if you can identify some person or some unit in the organization to whom you can address your request. If you cannot identify an individual, then address your letter to the Information Officer or the Director of Consumer Relations Department. Here is an example of such a letter:

> Dear Information Officer
>
> I am a Third Year B.Sc. Engineering student at Cathcart Polytechnic. As part of my course, I am doing a research project on computer-assisted design work in engineering. From reading articles in recent numbers of <u>New Engineering Journal</u>, I know that your company is in the forefront of that work.
>
> I would be grateful if you could send me information which is not confidential on the workings of the graphic generator model (Super 2), in particular, the application of this to bridge design.
>
> If it is not possible for you to comply with this request, I would appreciate any other material that you could supply, or suggest that I might read, on the application of computers to other aspects of engineering design.
>
> I enclose a stamped addressed envelope for your convenience.
>
> Thank you for your attention to my request.
>
> Yours faithfully
>
> R.B. Whataname

Your letter must create a favourable impression

Whatever the purpose of your letter, you want it to stand out from all the others being received. This is especially true of a letter of application for a job. For this reason, you must take care in the presentation of your message. Your facts must be accurate. Your spelling, punctuation and grammar must be correct. Your writing must be neat, conventionally spaced, and clearly readable. Your letter will create an impression of you as a person. Do everything you can to make that impression a favourable one.

THE CURRICULUM VITAE (C.V.)

Another document that you must prepare with careful attention to detail and layout is your curriculum vitae , which is Latin for 'course of life', i.e. your career to date. (The C.V. is known as a 'résumé' in certain international companies). It is a short, compact statement of your qualifications, education, work experience, publications, special interests or abilities, in addition to such vital statistics as your sex, age, birthday, marital status, and address, with a list of referees if required. The C.V. is usually submitted with a completed job application form and a covering letter explaining briefly why you are applying for a particular post.

Preparation of C.V.

It is advisable to have your C.V. typed, but if you can't do so, then neatly lay it out and write or print it legibly. Don't send photocopied C.V.'s to prospective employers, who will be more impressed by individualized documents. But be sure to keep a copy of your C.V., which you can update and modify as you gain new qualifications and/or experience.

Producing a good C.V. takes time and effort. You want to be sure that the information included is relevant to the job that you are seeking. This means that you may have to produce several different C.V.'s which will be suitable for different job applications.

Three questions to ask yourself

In preparing your C.V., ask yourself three basic questions about the information you are including:

1. Have you presented the reader with enough background information about yourself, e.g., education, training, work experience, etc?

2. Have you angled your achievements sufficiently towards the particular prospective employer?

3. Will the prospective employers be interested in these achievements, or will they perhaps want others that you have omitted?

Have someone else read over your work

Before posting your C.V. and letter of application, have a friend or a colleague read over both documents to check the writing, layout and kind of data presented. You may have made some mistakes in spelling or grammar, or made unjustifiable assumptions about what the prospective employer may or may not want to know about you, and your reader can suggest corrections or amendments.

There are no prescribed rules for the exact layout and wording of a C.V., but the following example is an acceptable form to use, subject to modifications where necessary:

NAME:	Jane Mary JONES	MARITAL STATUS:	Single
SEX:	Female	DATE OF BIRTH:	22 April 1965
NATIONALITY:	British		
HOME ADDRESS:	22 Bridge Avenue Small Town CATHCARTSHIRE CE6 1AX	TERM ADDRESS:	12 Hill Place GEORGETOWN GN5 4AP

EDUCATION [secondary school]

1977-82	Cathcart Academy, Cathcartshire
1981	SCE O Grades: Biology (A), Chemistry (B), English (A), French (C), Mathematics (B), Physics (B). (All summer exams)

1982	SCE Highers: Biology (B), Chemistry (A), English (B), Mathematics (C), Physics (A). (All summer exams)
1982	Georgetown College of Higher Education

B.Sc. Chemistry (Hons.), specializing in the chemistry of drugs — especially as applied to the treatment of arthritis in joints.

Expecting to graduate July 1986.

WORK EXPERIENCE

1972	Worked as shop assistant in Welcome Stores, Cathcart.
1983	Voluntary helper with Cathcart Youth Fellowship, organized holiday trips to coast and helped manager with administrative duties at the Fellowship Centre.
1984	Worked for four weeks in laboratories of Cathcart General Hospital as lab assistant (holiday relief).

SKILLS

Clean driving licence
Conversational French
Typing speed of 40 wpm

INTERESTS

Member of college folk club
Have taken part in college athletics — javelin. Member of college team.
Photography; do my own developing. Exhibited in local photographic show.

REFEREES

Mr C. Speed
Senior Lecturer
Department of Chemistry
Georgetown College of Higher
Education
GEORGETOWN
GN5 2AZ
Tel: 2782-2327896 (ext. 56)

Mrs D. Stuart
Leader
Cathcart Youth Fellowship
1 Park Road
CATHCART
CT7 1AB
Tel: 0990-5562453

APPLICATION FORMS

Here are eleven points to remember in completing a job application form:

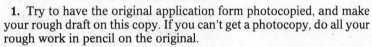

I'M THE GIRL FOR YOU!

1. Try to have the original application form photocopied, and make your rough draft on this copy. If you can't get a photocopy, do all your rough work in pencil on the original.

2. Follow the instructions on the application form exactly.

3. In writing your answers, stick to the boxes and spaces provided.

4. Never leave blanks. If you have no answer to give, mark the space 'Not Applicable' (or 'N/A').

5. If there is a space at the end of the form, in which you are invited to make a statement in support of your application, make good use of the opportunity to express your point of view. You may also have to use a separate sheet, which should be stapled to the application form.

Always write a first draft before completing the space on the form or the separate sheet. Check all your facts, and your English as well. Be truthful, and don't be too selective in reporting your ideas and the details of your life. At the same time, don't be afraid to 'angle' your information to suit the job you are seeking or to catch the interest of your reader.

6. Write down the information in a clear, bold manner, using a black-ink pen or biro, unless you have the form typed, in which case the typing should be legible and error-free.

7. Don't use unfamiliar abbreviations for courses or exams you have taken. Always provide an explanatory key.

8. Always say why you are applying for the particular job. Ask yourself: Why this job? Why am I the right person for it? Then answer these questions on the form.

9. Write a short covering letter to accompany your application form.

10. Before posting the form and your covering letter, check over them both one more time to ensure that you have not overlooked anything, such as your signature, or a date, or a referee's name and address, or a photograph of yourself if it is required.

11. Always keep copies of the completed application form and your covering letter for reference, and enclose an s.a.e. for a reply.

Application forms vary so greatly in layout and kinds of information requested that it would not be possible, or useful, to include a sample one here. But if you heed our suggestions, you will find completing an application form less laborious and bewildering. You will also produce a filled-in form that will probably stand out among all the other forms and thus attract the favourable attention of the prospective employer, whose interests and requirements you must always bear in mind when you complete the form.

SUMMARY OF THE MAIN POINTS

- The content and style of a letter should be appropriate to its purpose and the person or company to whom it is addressed.

- The three main types of letters are:
  1. personal
  2. official
  3. business

- Letters are written in two main layouts:
  1. semi-blocked
  2. blocked

- A curriculum vitae (C.V.), which is usually sent with a job application, is a compact personal history, including information on birth, sex, nationality, marital status, education, work experience, training, special interests or abilities, and referees.

- Fill in application forms neatly and clearly. Follow instructions and answer every question. Make sure you amplify and support your statement. Show why you are the right person for the job.

Further Reading

Gartside, L.   *Model Business Letters.*
                      Macdonald and Evans, 1981.

Thomson, K.G.   *The Pan Book of Letter Writing.*
                      Pan, 1965.

Woolcott, L. and   *Communication for Business and Secretarial*
W. Unwin.   *Students.* Macmillan, 1979.

Woolcott, L. and   *Mastering Business Communication.*
W. Unwin.   MacMillan, 1983.

Chapter 14 Examination Answers

Writing examination answers

Writing examination answers is a skill that can improve with practice. If you apply the common-sense suggestions that we offer you below, you may see benefit from them in higher grades, provided that you have done all the required study and revision before entering the examination hall. We also recommend that you look at the section on the exam essay in Chapter 11.

General advice

First, some general advice:

1. Read through the whole examination paper, noting all instructions on duration, number of questions to be answered, choice of sections, and the like.

2. Note the marks and amount of time allotted to each question.

3. If you have a choice of questions, select those which you think you can answer easily and quickly.

4. Answer only the question asked.

5. If you find that you can't finish the answer to a question, leave it and continue with the rest of the examination. You may be able to return to the question later and complete the answer.

6. Sufficient written explanation should accompany all numerical problems and proofs so that the examiner will know what you are doing.

7. As much as possible, use symbols rather than numbers in all your calculations, because they are more concise and more accurate.

8. Whenever you can, use diagrams in your solution to a problem, as they are often easier for an examiner to understand.

9. Write in clear, concise, legible English, and give all necessary details.

10. Don't cross out work unless you are sure it is wrong, as crossed-out work isn't marked.

11. Leave 10 minutes at the end of the examination period to clarify your diagrams, add footnotes or information to written answers, check calculations, and proofread your English.

12. Don't stop working before the end of the examination period.

Answering essay questions

Now, some advice applicable to answering essay-type examination questions:

1. Be sure that you completely understand each question. Underline on the exam paper all qualifying words and phrases, such as 'briefly', 'fully', 'in detail'. Be sure, too, that you know the meanings of the following directive words, which are among the most commonly used in examination questions. Here are some definitions, together with examples:

a. *compare:* to show similarities or differences in functions, qualities or characteristics. E.g.:

Compare the forms of mechanical support found in plants and animals.

b. *contrast:* to show differences in comparisons or when things are set side by side. E.g.:

Contrast the characters of Goneril and Regan with Cordelia in Shakespeare's *King Lear*.

c. *criticize:* to give a judgement about the value or truth of ideas, opinions, or facts, usually with supporting evidence. E.g.:

Criticize the reparations terms of the Treaty of Versailles.

d. *define:* to give the exact meaning of a term, theory, idea, or word, and note any distinctions or differences. E.g.:

Define 'decadence' as used by Friedrich Nietzsche.

e. *describe:* to represent by words or give an account of something. E.g.:

Describe the immediate and long-term effects of volcanic eruptions on a human population.

f. *discuss:* to examine by argument, presenting the various sides of a question or subject. E.g.:

Discuss the advantages and disadvantages of a parasitic mode of life.

g. *evaluate:* to estimate the value or amount of something, sometimes offering a personal opinion. E.g.:

Evaluate the importance of Platonic thought in Shelley's poetry.

h. *explain:* to make clear, to account for, or to interpret. E.g.:

Explain monetarist theory as propounded by Milton Friedman.

i. *illustrate:* to show by use of a figure or diagram, or to explain by representing concrete examples. E.g.:

Illustrate (with a diagram) how the two main tide-producing forces combine to produce variations in the height of tide.

j. *justify:* to present adequate reasons for conclusions or decisions. E.g.:

Justify the political and economic motives of the U.S. Government in building the Panama Canal.

k. *outline:* to show (often *briefly*) the key points or main ideas of a subject, stressing their arrangement and structure. E.g.:

Outline a method of surveying detail used in a plane table when the survey stations have been established and plotted on the plan.

l. *relate:* to show how facts or ideas are connected, and how much they are similar or influence each other (also, to tell a story). E.g.:

Relate the economic crisis in Europe of the 1920s to the rise of fascism in Germany.

m. *review:* to look over a subject, examining it critically. E.g.:

Review the development of the arms race between the U.S.A. and the U.S.S.R. from 1950 to 1985.

n. *summarize:* to give a short account of the main ideas or points of a subject, leaving out details and examples. E.g.:

Summarize the changes in British coinage over the past ten years.

o. *trace:* to show the development of a subject or idea. E.g.:

Trace the evolution of Freud's theory of the 'death wish' during the period following World War I.

2. Outline the main points that you want to include in your answer.

3. Don't write at great length on the questions you know a lot about just to impress the examiner.

4. Avoid wordiness.

5. Keep the wording of the question in mind.

6. Edit your information, selecting only what is relevant to put in your answer.

7. Never do less than the required number of answers. If you haven't time to write full answers for all the questions you are required to do, at least write some summary notes.

8. Present your facts and discussion in logical order in a continuous text with a beginning, a middle and an end, and with diagrams and calculations used as necessary.

9. Re-read your essay to check for mistakes in punctuation, spelling, grammar, also paying attention to clarity of expression and neatness of the text's appearance.

SUMMARY OF THE MAIN POINTS

■ Examination answers should be written exactly according to the instructions in the question, always keeping time and word limits in mind.

Further reading

Maddox, H.   *How to Study.* Pan, 1965.

Chapter 15 Giving an Effective Talk

Effective speaking, like effective writing, is a skill that can be acquired by practice. But it is difficult to develop the skill of effective speaking in a book. All we can do in this chapter is suggest ways in which you can help yourself to improve your speaking ability and recommend some techniques for preparing and delivering a short in-class talk.

Speaking and writing closely integrated

Effective speaking, like effective writing, depends on your abilty to organize and structure the words and sentences you wish to use. Don't think that speaking and writing are two separate divisions of communication. On the contrary, they are so closely integrated that to learn and practise the one is to learn and practise the other. But an effective writer will not always be an effective speaker, because there are psychological and temperamental circumstances which affect a speaker which do not affect a writer. Nonetheless, in many cases, the person who can organize and structure written material effectively will have an advantage when he or she has to speak to an audience.

Seven points to consider

To be an effective speaker, you should consider these seven important points, namely:

1. topic
2. language
3. audience
4. time
5. venue
6. audiovisual aids
7. preparation: organization and structure of material

Topic

The choice of topic is obviously important. It must be appropriate to the audience to whom you are going to speak. Whether you choose your own topic or it is assigned to you, always ask yourself what kind of information you will include in your talk and what kind of language you will use.

Language

You will use language to inform, or to explain, or to persuade. The language you use should be best suited to your audience. Choose your words carefully. Guard against using emotive or abusive language, such as slurs against religious, political or racial groups, which may arouse distrust, resentment, or other negative reactions in your audience.

Audience

Whenever possible, obtain information about the background, experience, interests, size and status of your audience. Ask yourself what they might want to know about your topic and how much they will already

know. It will be helpful to have some idea of what the audience expects from you, too. You will also want to know whether the members of the audience have been invited or are in compulsory attendance. Knowing what the occasion is — academic, recreational, social, or celebratory — will help you understand the audience's attitude to you, to your topic, and to the meeting itself, and help you select the right language and the right tone in your talk.

Time and freedom to alter it

You must know the date and hour of your talk, and how long you will be expected to speak. You may want to know, too, whether you have any freedom to alter the date, hour and length of your talk. Will there be any other speakers before or after you, or any other business to complete as in a meeting? It's important to know as well whether or not time will be allotted to a question-and-answer or discussion period at the end of your talk.

Venue and control of environment

There are many questions to consider concerning the place where your talk is to be given. Whether or not you have a choice in selecting the venue, you can at least find out what kind of venue it will be: classroom, hall, auditorium, lecturer's office, or wherever. It will help, of course, if the venue is familiar to you. Then you will know whether it is suitable for your audience and as an environment for your talk. If it is neither, perhaps you will be able to have the venue changed. You must know whether it is the right size for your audience. You don't want a room so small that people will be cramped in it, or so large that a small audience will feel lost in it.

Other questions to consider:

- Will there be enough seats for the audience?
- Will everyone be able to see you and your visual aids (if you are using them)?

- Will you be speaking from a dais, a platform, a lectern, a desk? Or will you be standing on the same level as the audience, or sitting down?
- Will everyone be able to hear you?
- Will there be enough room for the proper positioning of audiovisual equipment?
- Will you need a microphone, and is there a public address system?
- Will there be any disturbing noises in or near the venue, and will you be able to control them?
- Will there be the means to darken the venue easily to show slides or other visual aids?
- Will there be sufficient (or any) power points to use for audiovisual equipment?
- Will there be proper ventilation, heating and lighting as needed?

The venue is an important element contributing to the overall success of your talk. You may not, however, have any say in the arrangement for the venue or in controlling the environment, so you may have to make the best of the situation in which you find yourself. If at all possible, at least look over the venue beforehand and acquaint yourself with its essential features. If you are using audiovisual equipment requiring a darkened room, you may need an assistant to help you with drawing blinds and switching lights off and on.

Audiovisual aids

You must plan the use of audiovisual aids very carefully. Just moving them from one place to another can present problems. Before undertaking the use of these aids, you will first want to find out what equipment can be made available to you, such as, film, video tapes, sound tapes (battery-run or power outlet), slides, overhead projectors, and three-dimensional models for demonstration purposes. Remember, too, that visual aids may also be charts, drawings, posters and blackboard diagrams which you will have to prepare in advance. In any case, you must decide whether the aids will really enhance your talk, or detract from it.

Points to consider using
audiovisual aids

If you use audiovisual aids, here are ten points to consider:

1. Keep charts, posters, display cards, etc., simple. Use big, bold, clear lettering. Emphasize only important details.

2. Allow time for the audience to absorb information.

3. Use a few well presented visuals rather than many, which might distract or confuse the audience.

4. Explain the layout, elements and meaning of your display.

5. Give the source of the information you use.

6. Test your audiovisual equipment before you use it in your talk.

7. Remember to provide ventilation in the venue when blinds are drawn.

8. Check that your slides are clean and the right way up.

9. Check on spare bulbs, leads, and other extra equipment which you might need.

10. Test tapes, sound levels, etc., on the audio equipment before using it.

Partnership of
speaker and audience

Your talk is a partnership between you and your audience. To make the partnership a happy and successful one, the most important quality you can have is enthusiasm for your topic, which you will try to share with your audience. Make your purpose clear and easy to understand, and never apologize to your audience by using such expressions as 'Unaccustomed as I am to public speaking' and 'I'm afraid I've not had much time to prepare this talk.' Come fully prepared, with enthusiasm for your topic and confidence in yourself, and your partnership with the audience will be a mutually beneficial one.

Preparing your talk:
clear structure

Give your listeners a clear structure to follow. They will not only find listening to you easier but they will also be more likely to remember the material and to ask you questions about it afterwards. Tell them what you are going to do, and how you are going to do it, and then do it.

Choice of structures

Your talk must have a clear, solid structure, basically a beginning (introduction), a middle (development), and an end (conclusion). Within this basic arrangement, you have a choice of using one or more of several different ways to organize your material, such as:

The narrative

This tells a story. The personal narrative is good for a report on a holiday, a journey, or an interesting experience, which you can enliven with anecdotes and humour.

The chronological narrative

In this, you follow a time sequence in relating the story, useful for the personal narrative as well as for historical or biographical topics or for topics dealing with the development of a theory, an experiment, or a product.

Here is an example of the use of the chronological structure in a talk by a personnel officer of a large firm to representatives of each department. His topic is the origin and development of the idea of flextime at work places:

- Flextime Origins: — West Germany in early 1960s

    — Rapid spread through Europe and U.S.A.

    — Over 200,000 applications in U.K. by mid 1970s

- Present Day: — Examples of main types of flextime

    — Core time/full-time division

    — Main advantages

    — Problems in implementation

- Future: — Increased leisure?

    — Increased demand for family time?

    — Quote examples from Sweden

    — 'Robot' revolution; need for full-time to use machines to best advantage

The analytical

This is the best structure to use for the informative talk, following this general arrangement of the sections:

- *Introduction:*

    a. Tell your audience your aims in the talk.

    b. Give a brief survey of the topic, then tell your audience you will concentrate on only three or four aspects or themes.

    c. Introduce a short chronological sequence (as above) to set the topic in a time scale for your audience.

- *Development:*

  a. Deal with each of your aspects or themes in turn, spending some time on theory, and using specific examples.

- *Conclusion:*

  a. Review the more important points you have made, and give your considered opinion as to their significance.

Suppose the personnel manager mentioned above was asked to give his talk to the supervisory staff on the possibility of introducing flextime into their company, and consider its main advantages and disadvantages. The analytical structure of his talk might look like this:

- *Introduction:*

a. aims of the talk: to show advantages and disadvantages of flextime

b. brief survey of the recent growth of flextime
(see chronology above)

- *Development:*

a. theme **(i):**   flextime helps combat congestion

      — getting to and from work

      — use of facilities (e.g., canteen, toilets)

      — quote example from local firm

b. theme **(ii):**   flextime depends on good organization of 'core time'

      — theoretical: use overhead projector

      — practical: example from West Germany

      — studies done in one department of firm

c. theme **(iii):**   flextime disadvantages

      — contacting people from non-flextime firms

      — coping with sudden production emergencies

      — example of initial problems from local firm

- *Conclusion:*

a. flextime as part of wider campaign to increase job satisfaction

b. flextime as part of wider campaign to improve attendance at work

c. personal view: sum up on advantages and disadvantages, especially for the firm, and give opinion on its feasibility in the firm.

Notice that the speaker used a brief chronology in the introduction before developing his remarks on the three themes, in which he analysed the points for and against flextime. In addition, notice that the speaker balanced the theoretical aspects with concrete examples in the development section. Audiences generally like to have definite facts and examples to think about and discuss in question time.

The logical

See also Chapter 9. This is a method recommended for organizing a persuasive or argumentative talk, in which you aim to win your audience over to your point of view or cause. In constructing logical arguments, you will want to consider which of the following methods would best suit your purpose:

- *The inductive:*

    a. Observe the facts, and note the background to them, then state the generalization based on them.

    b. Test this method by asking:

    i. Are the facts relevant?

    ii. Are the facts sufficient?

    iii. Are there exceptions to the facts as given?

- *The deductive:*

    a. State the generalization and deduce particulars from it.

    b. Test this method by asking:

    i. Is the generalization valid?

    ii. Is there a logical connection between the particulars and the generalization?

- *The analogous:*

    a. Draw a comparison between two terms known to be similar in some respects, assuming that they are similar in one particular characteristic.

    b. Test this method by asking:

    i. Are the comparisons relevant?

    ii. Are the comparisons fair?

- *The cause and effect:*

    a. Attribute an effect to a certain cause.

    b. Test this method by asking:

    i. Is the cause not the effect of some other cause?

    ii. Are cause and effect not themselves both effects of some other cause and not directly related at all?

Other structures

In addition to the methods of structuring your talk listed above, you can also:

- Point out facts for and against an issue.
- Proceed from the unimportant to the important items-
- Proceed from the easy (e.g., $2 + 2 = 4$) or familiar to the difficult (e.g., $x^9\sqrt{2y^2 - n}$) or unfamilair.

Provide a conclusion

Whichever method or combination of methods you choose, always provide a definite conclusion to your talk, in which you can either summarize the key points for your audience or emphasize certain ideas for future discussion. In some cases, it might be advisable to do both in your conclusion.

Preparing yourself for your talk

Do not read your talk to your audience. Instead, write out the talk in full to begin with, if you wish, but condense this full text into notes which you can write on handy cards or a few small sheets of paper. Your notes will help you remember what comes next in the planned sequence of your talk. Leave wide margins on both sides of the cards or sheets. Print boldly or type your notes. For example, Figs. 1 and 2 show one way of laying out notes on two cards, relating to the topic of electronic mail systems in a twelve-minute in-class talk.

Notice that the left-hand margins are reserved to mark approximate timing per numbered heading, to indicate where you are, or ought to be in your talk. You might also want to allow time for questions or discussion at the end of your talk, as this speaker has done. In the right-hand margins are brief notes to remind you of things you must do during the talk, such as show an overhead projector slide, display a chart, quote from a text. The reminders may be necessary, for the pressures of giving a talk can sometimes cause you to miss out something important which you intend to include.

Delivery
Eye contact

Look at your audience as much as possible. By doing so, you will encourage your listeners to give you their full attention, and you will find it easier to judge how well or badly you are doing. Look at all the members of the audience, not just at those in front of you. Don't look out of a window, or at the ceiling, or at the floor, or at the back wall. If you lose eye contact with your listeners, you risk losing their interest.

APPROX. TIMING: MINUTES	TOPIC: ELECTRONIC MAIL SYSTEMS Card 1	AUDIOVISUAL ACTION
1	1. Introduction	Overhead Projector (OHP) 1
2	2. Advantages	OHP 2
2	3. Disadvantages	Chart A

Fig. 1   Card 1 of notes for in-class talk

APPROX. TIMING: MINUTES	Card 2	AUDIOVISUAL ACTION
2	4. Costs Model A £— £—	OHP 3
2	Model B £— £—	OHP 4
3	5. Future Development	Quotation
12 Mins.	Time for questions/discussion?	

Fig. 2   Card 2 of notes for in-class talk

Voice control

Vary your voice without distracting your audience. Consider the pace of your speaking, tone of voice, emphasis on words, and volume. You may have to adjust the volume of your voice to the acoustics of the room and the size of the audience. Project your voice to the back of the room, but don't shout; to project your voice effectively, try to produce your voice from your chest rather than your throat. If you have a naturally soft voice, you will need to be especially conscious of audibility. Make sure that your articulation of words is clear. Don't rush your words, mumble or mutter. Avoid starting your sentences with 'um', smacking your lips, repeatedly clearing your throat, swallowing your words, dropping your volume at the end of sentences, talking and laughing at the same time, and peppering your talk with monotonous and irritating 'ah's' after every other word. Learn to control your voice; no one else can do so for you.

Posture, stance, use of hands

Be careful of your posture. Avoid slouching or stooping. By standing up straight, but not stiffly, you will give your voice a better chance to be heard. Find a comfortable, natural stance for yourself. Don't shuffle your feet or gesture with your hands unless you have a good reason for doing so, such as emphasizing a point with a motion of your hand. But use gestures sparingly; don't let your hands do your 'talking' for you. Don't put your hands in your pockets where you might be tempted to jingle coins or keys. The best place to keep your hands is at your sides as much as possible, when you are not engaged in operating audiovisual aids or pointing to a chart.

Nervousness

If you suffer from nervousness — and most speakers do to some degree — work out a procedure to help you relieve your tension and relax before you start to speak. For instance, you might take deep breaths, review your notes, or rehearse your opening remarks. But the best preventive measure against nervousness is thorough preparation of your talk.

Sometimes you may feel nervous because you are afraid of making a mistake or forgetting an important point or doing something embarrassing, especially if you are speaking to an audience composed of classmates and friends. If you make a mistake or forget a point, say so, and don't panic. The world won't end, and your audience will probably admire you for your honesty in admitting the error of fact or the lapse of memory.

How to prepare a short talk

We will now show you, step by step, how to prepare a short talk. You should be able to use this method for almost any kind of talk or presentation of whatever length, although, of course, the longer the talk, the more time and work must be invested in preparing it.

Let's suppose you are asked to give a twelve-minute in-class talk on a subject related to your degree subject, which, let's say, is chemistry. The topic you choose is an aspect of computing, namely, on-line computer-assisted database retrieval, which interests you and which you think will also interest your classmates.

First step: gathering ideas in spider-web form

Your first step is to take a large sheet of paper and firmly write the topic of your talk in the centre. Then, for half an hour, you jot down in spider-web form around the centre any ideas relating to the topic as they occur to you. You use the spider web, as illustrated in Fig. **3**, because it allows you to see more easily how ideas relate to each other than does a simple list of ideas.

You keep adding to this spider web over the following few days. Having checked through reference books on computers and information technology, you will have enough material to fill up spider webs on two sheets of paper. You stop researching at this point, recalling the twelve-minute time limit on your talk.

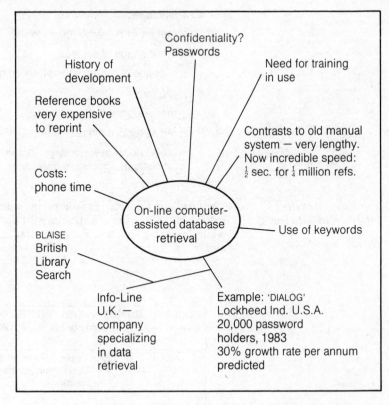

Fig. 3   General spider web on talk topic

Second step: shaping ideas into a structure

Your second step, after gathering the ideas, is to organize them into a clear, definite structure which will be easy for your audience to follow. Since you intend to give an informative talk, you choose the analytical method of organizing your ideas as we outlined above. When you cut out all the irrelevant ideas, and order the remaining material into an analytical structure, the arrangement might look like this:

Analytical structure

- History:
  - development of databases and computer-based retrieval
  - the BLAISE (British Library Search) project
- How it works
  - keywords
  - unlocking pathways
  - example from Chemical Database
- Costs
  - paying to subscribe to a database
  - telephone and computer time
  - example: DIALOG, U.S.A.

- Advantages
  - — rapidity of research (quote facts)
  - — combination of sources
  - — expense of buying new reference books
- The future
  - — more databases (Info-Line U.K.)
  - — prices reduced in real terms
  - — professional use: doctors, teachers, farmers
    (Ministry of Agriculture database)

Third step: transfer
information onto cards

The third and final step in your preparation is to transfer all the information contained in your structure list onto cards, which you can use while delivering your talk. Examples of such cards are shown in Figs. 4, 5 and 6.

TIMING: MINUTES	TOPIC: ON-LINE COMPUTER-ASSISTED DATABASE RETRIEVAL Card 1	AUDIOVISUAL ACTION
2	1. History: — development of database and computer-based retrieval	OHP: BLAISE project
3	2. How it works: keywords unlocking pathways example from Chemical Database	Blackboard diagram

Fig. 4   Card 1 of notes for in-class talk

TIMING: MINUTES	Card 2	AUDIOVISUAL ACTION
2	3. Costs: — paying to subscribe to database telephone and computer time — example: DIALOG, U.S.A.	Chart A
2	4. Advantages: — rapidity of search (quote facts) — combination of sources — expense of buying new reference books	

Fig. 5   Card 2 of notes for in-class talk

TIMING: MINUTES	Card 3	AUDIOVISUAL ACTION
3	5. The future: — more databases Info-Line U.K. prices reduced in real terms — professional use by doctors, teachers, farmers (Ministry of Agriculture database)	Chart B
12 Mins.	Time for questions/discussion?	

Fig. 6   Card 3 of notes for in-class talk

SUMMARY OF THE MAIN POINTS

■ A speaker's first aim is to hold the listeners' interest and attention by means of eye contact, voice control, and enthusiasm for the topic.

■ A speaker must always consider the type of audience, venue, audio-visual aids, and provide clear, definite and easy-to-follow organization of material.

■ A speaker should rehearse the talk once or twice before delivering it to the audience.

■ Thorough preparation is the best way for a speaker to prevent nervousness.

Further Reading

Goodworth, C.   *Effective Speaking and Presentation for the Business Executive.* Business Books, 1980.

Mackay, C.   *Speak for Yourself.* Gower Press, 1971.

Mears, A.G.   *The Right Way to Speak in Public* Paperfront Books, 1977.

Wilson, J. and C. Arnold.   *Dimensions of Public Communication.* Allyn and Bacan (U.S.A.), 1976.

Wood, M.   *The Art of Speaking.* David and Charles, 1971.

Chapter 16   Listening and Note Taking

Listening, the neglected communication skill

Note taking

Handouts?

Poor lecture notes

Listening is the most neglected communication skill. It is the one that is most used — students regularly spend up to 70 per cent of their 'working week' listening — and yet the one which is seldom taught or developed.

Many companies are actively involved with programmes on listening skills for their staff, and new attention is being paid to the development of listening skills in classroom and lecture hall.

The first point to note is that good listening is not the same as hearing. We can hear something but the sound fails to register; we have to be actively listening. Listening is not a passive business, it is an active process and can be very hard work indeed. Sitting actively listening to talks and lectures all day is very exhausting.

We shall now try to identify some of the criteria that go to make for better listening. These are broad generalities and may not apply in all circumstances.

Active listening usually means having some system for recording the information that is coming in. Most people forget up to 75 per cent of a talk or lecture within the space of twenty-four hours; having a reliable and efficient 'recording' system helps reduce that loss considerably.

Taking notes from a text is a simple matter compared with the difficulty of note taking during the lecture. (One can always take in a cassette recorder, but think of the 'decoding job' at the end of all the lectures!) Unlike working with a text, the lecturer doesn't allow you to turn back; you have to keep up with the pace, points come and go, references are made and examples given. How do you record it all — or even a fraction of it — for your own eventual benefit?

Lecturers vary widely in their technique. Some provide full handouts, but you are advised to add details and other notes to these as the lecturer proceeds — then you will remain an active listener, not a merely passive one content to rest knowing you have the handout. Most times you will have to act on your own initiative, and you will have to decide when to make notes.

There are as many ways of note taking as there are ways of lecturing. We have touched on some of these methods in our chapter on retrieval of information. Which ever method you use, the acid test is whether you can follow your own notes after a few days and recall the key points of the lecture or discussion.

On the next page (Fig. 1) are some sample notes that a student took while listening to the introductory remarks of a lecture on soil development in a geography course.

> SOIL STRUCTURE
> HUMUS → ORGANIC, WEATHERING MATERIAL
> MIXTURE ORGANIC — INORGANIC — CLAY
> HUMUS COMPLEX — SOIL FERTILITY
> MICELLES   PREVENTS
>   / RAIN LEACHING
> SOIL SKELETON SALTS

Fig. 1   Sample of rough lecture notes

How much of the above will be meaningful to the student a day or a week after the lecture? Will it be useful to the student during revision for an examination?

Notes which are clearly laid out and logically organized on the page are likely to be of more value for revision and for helping the student gain a better understanding of the material.

Improved lecture notes

Consider the example in Fig. 2 (next page). The notes are the same but compare the treatment with that above.

Notice that the student has spaced, ordered and numbered the several parts of this introductory material. The diagram is larger, more visible and therefore more memorable. Abbreviations are still used, but there are enough key statements to impress the structure of the lecture firmly in the student's mind. The student has also dated the page. It is a small but significant addition, for the chronological sequence of lecture notes may be of importance in understanding the development of the ideas. Get into the habit of dating your notes, reports and other documents.

Fig. 2   Sample of improved lecture notes

The POKEEARS system

In his booklet *Learning from Lectures,* Dr George Brown of Nottingham University has devised a system to help students sharpen their listening skills. It is designed to encourage them to be active rather than passive listeners; to be able to gauge what is happening; and to put them into a state of readiness for active participation and note taking.

Most lectures and talks have some kind of pattern. First, there is usually an introduction or preamble which sets the scene. This is followed by identification of the topic, key points, examples, asides, reservations and a summary which rounds off the lecture and perhaps indicates the topic of the next one. Not all lectures conform to this pattern, but many do, and most will have some kind of structure that can be decoded with the help of POKEEARS.

These are the eight points of POKEEARS (Preamble, Orientation, Key points, Extensions, Examples, Asides, Reservations, Summaries).

1. Preamble. This usually consists of preliminary remarks — greetings, reminders of assignments due, references to previous lectures.

2. Orientation. Any remarks which introduce the lecture proper, or the topics or subtopics of the lecture, e.g., 'Now let's look at . . .', or, 'Today we are going to look at . . .'. This usually occurs after a preamble but it may be embedded in the preamble.

3. Key points. An important statement of facts, concepts, values, principles, processes or procedures. A key point may often be regarded as the answer to a specific question. Sometimes key points occur in clusters. Sometimes key points may be major or minor. If you are not sure if a statement is a key or not, it is better to code it as a key.

4. Extensions. The key point is interpreted, extended or elaborated upon. Sometimes two key points may be linked through an extension. Common opening phrases are, 'That is to say . . .', or, 'Put it another way . . .', or, 'This may be regarded as . . .'.

5. Examples. Examples, illustrations, metaphors or analogies are used to introduce a key point, to explain a key point or reinforce a key point. In such instances the lecturer may use such phrases as, 'For example . . .', or, 'Let me give you an illustration of what I mean . . .'.

6. Asides. These may contain material which is interesting but not crucial. Asides may be anecdotes. They may be virtually irrelevant. Asides may begin with, 'Incidentally . . .', or 'By the way . . .' etc. They often end with, 'Be that as it may . . .', or, 'However, let's get back to . . .'.

7. Reservations. Reservations and qualifications made to the main points or to the examples cited, e.g., 'However, this is, of course, not a perfect analogy', or, 'But one should be wary of . . .'.

8. Summaries. Any remarks which summarize the lecture, topic or sub-topic of a lecture.

● **Unclassifiable.** Any remarks or actions which do not fit the above categories, e.g., lecturer scrambling through notes, unimportant statement about weather, football, etc.

Ask yourself questions

Another way to be an active listener is to ask yourself questions about the lecture or discussion while it is in progress. Jot down these questions in the margins of your notes, and raise them when there is an oppor-

tunity to do so. Never hesitate to ask your lecturer, or the speaker, for explanations, clarifications or points of additional information. It's the most convincing way to prove that you *have* been listening, and it will certainly encourage the speaker.

Discipline your thinking

In asking yourself questions and noting them down, there is a danger that you will stop listening to the lecturer and become absorbed in your own thoughts. Such speculations are not bad — in fact they may be rewarding, but you should try to discipline your thoughts to stay on the subject matter to hand.

Reflection, and putting material into patterns

Active listening is not only questioning yourself, it is also reflecting on what else you may know about the subject and how the new material fits into it. Both alertness and concentration are improved for those students who try and fit the new information into some sort of pattern with their previously acquired knowledge.

Listen for content

The 'good' listener is concerned with the content and is not put off too much by the delivery. Of course, no one enjoys listening to a dull or irritating voice. If, however, you want to become a better, and more active, listener, you will learn to ignore unappealing delivery, as well as any quirks or eccentricities the lecturer has that might distract you from the actual content.

Be selfish

Be selfish here. Ask yourself about the lecture, 'What's in it for me?' The answer is simple: to get as much information or understanding out of the lecture as possible. Everything else is irrelevant to this all-important purpose.

Facts and ideas

Some students listen mainly for facts. They are so busy writing down the facts in their notebooks that they often overlook the main ideas presented in the lecture or discussion. Facts can be checked in a textbook, but ideas, especially if they are original with the speaker, may not be so easy to trace or pin down elsewhere. When you're listening, identify the main ideas and central thoughts (the POKEEARS system will help you to do so), underlining them or writing them in block capitals for emphasis and memorability.

Do something constructive with notes

It's pointless to become a better listener and note taker if, after the lecture or discussion, you don't do something constructive with your notes. As soon as possible after the lecture, certainly before the day is passed, try to:

- File them into subject, topic order, if reasonably legible.
- Write out the main points or key statements in a more legible hand.

The very act of doing this will help imprint the material into your memory.

Listening is a complex skill, still much underrated. We have presented you with some suggestions on how to learn to improve your skill in listening with increased personal profit in lectures, tutorials and seminars. It is a skill that judging from surveys of employers is valued greatly by them from would-be candidates to jobs. It is a skill that brings you friends ('I can talk to John, he can really listen').

Good listening is not only a highly developed skill, it is also active participation in the communication experience.

Ignore any eccentricities of the lecturer.

SUMMARY OF THE MAIN POINTS

- Good listening is not just hearing; it is an active process at which one works hard.

- Good listening can be achieved by not being distracted by the delivery of the speaker.

- The good listener will go for ideas not just facts. A system such as POKEEARS may be used.

- The good listener will have a note-taking system and not trust to memory.

LISTENING AND NOTE TAKING

Further Reading

Allen, M.B. *Listening the Forgotten Skill.*
Wiley, 1982.

Brown, G. *Learning from Lectures.*
University of Nottingham, 1979.

Ferguson, N. *Listening and Note Taking.*
CEEL Press, 1977.

Chapter 17 Improving Your Reading Skills

Reading: visual and mental

Reading is, first, a visual process, involving skilled eye movements that take in the printed symbols (words) — a complex communication code — and, second, a mental process whereby the symbols are decoded and translated into meaning. This skill in reading has taken you many years of practice to acquire.

The reading process: the eye

Your eye moves from left to right along the line of print in quick jerks with pauses (fixations) in between, then swings from the right end to the left end to begin the next line of print.

Reading a line of easy text about 4″ (10 cm) long, you make five or six pauses, but more if the text is difficult. Eye movements between pauses take up about 10 per cent of your reading time; the length of each pause is about 0.25 second. The number of regressions (as the eye looks back at words previously read) is less than one.

The amount of text you take in while reading depends on your recognition span, and on the length of the pauses. You can see about two words clearly, with a blurry impression of one or two more in your side or peripheral vision, so that you take in three or four connected words in about 0.25 second. Since there are usually only ten or twelve words per 4″ line of printed text, you can read it in three or four pauses.

The reading process: the mind

Reading is possible only when you are already familiar with the language, and to become familiar with it has also taken you many years of practice.

You read familiar words, idioms, phrases and sentences as wholes, reacting to them as units of expression. The printed words trigger off habits of speech, and you can usually anticipate what is coming next in the passage, because you already know the grammatical structure of the sentence through your familiarity with the language.

Skipping parts of text

Reading a light novel or a newspaper story, you will not, if you are a skilled reader, read every word of every sentence or paragraph. You will skip a great deal of the text, and yet, being well acquainted with the language, mentally piece together a more or less coherent idea of the content based partly on the printed word and partly on previous reading experience.

Knowing the purpose of a text

Knowing the purpose of a text not only helps you in reading and understanding it, but also in anticipating its structure. A title, such as 'The Rights and Wrongs of Euthanasia', may offer a clue: you will expect to read about arguments for and against mercy killing. Furthermore, when you read the contents page of a report, for example, you expect to see some indication of a structure, in the form of introduction, main body, conclusion, and recommendations. Since such a structure guides your reading, you are mentally better prepared to comprehend the material. Thus, if you can pick out the structure of a text, and anticipate its direction, you will find the reading task easier.

Reasons to read

It is important to know why you are reading a text. The main reasons are summarized in the following categories:

1. To get a quick impression of a text by scanning, for example, a list of chapter titles, or names in a telephone directory. Scanning is a method to pick up key facts, or to sort out the relevant material from the irrelevant, and is useful in preparing for the reading of a long or difficult text.

2. To get a general view of a book by skimming through it. Skimming is exploratory reading, at a slower speed than in scanning. You are searching for headings, sub-headings, titles, paragraph topic sentences, summaries of chapters or sections in a textbook. Concern is with individual paragraphs and pages, and so more detail is taken in.

3. To master information, such as a difficult text book or a reference work, which requires slow, careful, and often repeated readings.

4. To revise a text to confirm your knowledge of the content of a book or your own lecture notes in preparation for an exam.

5. To search for specific information, as when you are conducting research for a report, or to answer a question by consulting an encyclopaedia or a dictionary.

6. To criticize a text, as when you have to write a book review, a literary critique, or a précis of a passage, and when you are taking notes on a text.

7. To proofread, which requires that you pay meticulous and close attention to spelling, punctuation, grammar, factual accuracy, layout, etc., before submitting an essay or a report for a grade.

8. To enjoy a text, as in reading a novel, or to get the gist of a newspaper article, when your reading speed will be very fast.

In short, you must be flexible in your reading methods and speeds, according to the reason you are reading and the kind of text you are reading. Flexible reading is efficient reading.

Poor readers

Poor readers often read each word, while good readers take in whole three-to-four-word sections of a line of print. The longer the poor readers linger over a word, the slower their reading rate will be. Not only do they read each word, but they also re-read words (regression).

To show you what we mean let us take the first few lines of Constance Trescot's essay on language which we included in our chapter on the essay.

A poor reader might approach the text in this way:

There have | been many | hopes | that the | human race |
might | achieve | greater unity | by having | one common |
language | to speak | instead of the | 2000 | or so | now |
spoken. | Before the 16th | century | , Latin | was the |
dominant language | of Europe | . It crossed | all |
boundaries | , and it was | the international | tongue |
spoken by | educated persons | regardless | of their |
national origins | . . .

We see that the reader has paused very many times, and that relatively
few phrases and word groups have been read in a single sweep of the eye.
Also notice that this reader has the habit of stopping at the end of each
line despite the fact that there are no full stops at the end of any line.
Compare it to this approach:

There have been many hopes | that the human race |
might achieve greater unity | by having one common
language to speak | instead of the 2000 or so now
spoken. | Before the 16th century | , Latin was the
dominant language of Europe | . It crossed all
boundaries | , and it was the international tongue
spoken by educated persons | regardless of their
national origins | . . .

Here we can see that this reader has taken in many more phrases and
word groups with wider sweeps of the eye. Notice too that the reader
has not stopped at the end of each line, but followed the flow of the text.

The speed of reading

The speed of reading depends as much on familiarity with the material
and reading experience as on physical eye movements, which are symp-
toms, not causes, of difficulties in reading. The number of eye movements per line is important, but so is the amount of time for which your
eye stops moving. Considering the eye alone, and allowing for the times
between pauses, it is possible for you to increase your reading rate.

Your reading rate depends on the easiness or difficulty of the text and
on the purpose of your reading it. For example, you may read a spy novel
for entertainment at about 200-plus words per minute, but read a single
paragraph of a complex science or engineering textbook four or five
times before you grasp its meaning. It is important not only to read
rapidly, but also to understand what you are reading.

*Calculating your
reading rates*

To calculate your reading rates, take sample passages from several
different kinds of text — a light novel, a newspaper or magazine, a textbook — and count the words in each selected passage, time yourself
reading each one, then by dividing the number of words in each by the
time for each, find your rates in words per minute.

Some slow readers may also be good readers, while some fast readers
may be poor readers. What matters most is how much of the material
that you read you can understand and recall, not sheer reading speed in
itself.

But if your reading rate of easy material is under 200 words per
minute, you should try to learn to read more quickly. You can't speak
faster than about 125 words per minute, but you should be able to read
two to three times that many words in the same time.

Reasons for
slow reading

First, find out what causes your slow reading. Among the reasons may be one or more of the following:

- spelling out words letter by letter
- finger pointing
- reading word by word
- moving your lips as you read
- making sub-vocal sounds
- re-reading words along the line of print
- having an inadequate vocabulary
- having a habit of slow reading regardless of type of material
- having difficulty with return sweep to the next line

To increase your
reading rate

Next, to increase your reading rate, organize a daily period of systematic practice in reading for three or four weeks. Estimate the number of words in selected texts, and time yourself in reading each one. Start with short, easy passages from daily newspapers or a popular magazine. After about two weeks of this practice, you will probably notice that your new reading rate has stabilized at about 100 words per minute faster than the beginning rate. Include vertical scanning in your practice.

Then extend this practice to more difficult material, such as a textbook. It will help you, too, if you keep records of your reading material and reading rates for different kinds of texts, technical and scientific, literary and historical, since the former usually have to be read more slowly than the latter. You might like to construct a graph to record the increase in your reading rates as you practise.

AND WHAT MR·DESCARTES, DO YOU THINK YOU MEAN BY "I AM"

'Think of questions you would like to ask the author if he or she were in your company.'

Suggestions to improve concentration, increase comprehension

To help you improve your ability to concentrate on more difficult texts and increase your comprehension of them, here are a few suggestions to bear in mind:

1. Know why you are reading. Ask yourself: What do I want to get out of this textbook?

2. Do not remain a passive spectator of the printed page. Ask yourself: What angle does this writer have?

3. Read a difficult text at least two or three times, and then jot down the main points or facts from each paragraph, often provided in the topic or summary sentence. You might also phrase a few questions you'd like to ask the author if he or she were in your company as you read the book. Read critically.

4. Make sure you have a general plan to your reading that you follow consistently.

5. Avoid bias or prejudice in your opinions of the text. Try to be objective.

Your reading environment

In addition, it is important that you have a good reading environment, although if you are living in digs or in halls of residence, you can't always control your environment satisfactorily. At the very least you should have adequate lighting and ventilation, a reasonably comfortable chair to sit in while reading, and a writing place nearby, and you should be free of unwanted distractions as far as is possible. Some

students can work well with music playing, for instance, while others need total quiet — this is a personal choice. Finally, obey signs of fatigue and failing concentration. If your eyes and mind are tired, you will waste your time if you continue reading. Take a rest, or do something else completely different from reading.

Inadequate vocabulary

If the reason you read slowly is that you fail to recognize and understand the meanings of some of the words in a text, then you may want to take steps to increase your vocabulary.

Kinds of vocabulary

The average student at college or university has about 3,000 words in his or her everyday vocabulary, called the working vocabulary. Besides these words, the student will probably have a recognition vocabulary of about 2,000 words, whose meaning is more or less clear from the contexts in which they appear, but which are not generally used in the student's common speech or writing exercises. Beyond these two vocabularies, the student may encounter unfamiliar words in particular disciplines, such as, technological, scientific, sociological and the like, many of which are of Greek or Latin origin, and may pose problems for the student who has never seen them before.

Ways to improve your vocabulary

The best way to improve your vocabulary is to read widely in your own area or areas of study. Real understanding of word usage comes from seeing words used in a variety of contexts.

Other ways to improve your vocabulary are:

1. to look up unfamiliar words in a good dictionary
(see chapter on spelling and dictionaries for further details)

2. to use new words in your speech and writing

3. to prepare a glossary of the technical terms used in your area or areas of study, and master this special vocabulary

4. to devise a system of alphabetical cards on which you record new words with their definitions, synonyms, and derivations
(see the chapter on spelling and dictionaries for guidance)

5. to draw up a list of some prefixes and suffixes commonly used in English to help you understand compound words
(see chapter on spelling and dictionaries for a sample list).

Reading: your most important study skill

Reading is probably the most important study skill you possess. Your ultimate aim is to read critically and with a purpose. The success of any attempt you make to increase your reading speed depends largely on your own interest and motivation in achieving this goal.

Good reading: effective strategy

Good reading is having an effective strategy, an overall plan of approach. This means that you must know why you are reading, and what you hope to get out of reading.

Question yourself and the author as you read. The questioning will help you remember what you read, as you will become an active reader, instead of remaining passive.

Finally, to help impress the material in your memory, take notes on the author's main points. As one Chinese proverb puts it, 'The palest ink is better than the most retentive memory.' In this way, too, you will become more of a participant in the act of reading.

SUMMARY OF THE MAIN POINTS

■ Reading skills improve with practice.

■ Reading speeds vary according to the type of text and whether its style and content are difficult or easy.

■ Reading speed can be increased by increasing the range of each eye movement, and by increasing vocabulary.

Further Reading

Deleeuw, M.   *Read Better, Read Faster.*
               Pelican, 1965.

Maddox, H.   *How to Study.* Pan, 1965.

Main, A.   *Encouraging Effective Learning.*
               Scottish Academic Press, 1980.

Reid, J.   *A Guide to Effective Study,*
               2nd ed. University of Edinburgh, n.d.

Conclusion Fourteen Points to Remember

In summary of the main ideas on improving your skills in writing, speaking, listening and reading, which we have presented and developed in this handbook, here are some key points and suggestions to bear in mind:

1. Your ideal in both writing and speaking is the four C's: be clear, correct, concise and coherent.

2. Always be conscious of your readers' and listeners' needs, interests and knowledge.

3. Organize your written works and talks with a beginning, a middle and an end, and structure your material according to a clear, definite and easy-to-follow method.

4. Keep your graphs, charts, tables and diagrams simple, clear, accurate and direct.

5. Acquire a good dictionary and make full use of it. We recommend the *Collins English Dictionary*. We also suggest that you acquire a copy of the *New Collins Thesaurus* to help you improve your vocabulary.

6. Acquaint yourself with your institutional or municipal library and learn to use its services and facilities.

7. Your listening and note-taking skills may be improved by use of the POKEEARS system: Preamble, Orientation, Key Points, Extensions, Examples, Asides, Reservations, Summaries.

8. Increase your reading skills by increasing your vocabulary and the speed of your eye movements.

9. Always ask whether your department or institution has a 'house style' to guide you in preparing written work and talks before following the styles we have suggested.

10. Essays, reports and letters should go through two drafts as you correct, improve and polish your work.

11. Develop the practice of being critical as you check over your writing for accuracy in content and layout. Proofread for mistakes in spelling, grammar and punctuation.

12. Take care to produce neat, tidy and attractive-looking essays, reports and letters, which will help give the impression of professionalism and competence.

13. Always keep copies of your essays, reports and important business letters for your files or for future reference.

14. Be flexible; adapt our suggestions, advice and instructions to suit your own needs and circumstances.

Good luck and good grades!

R.E. & K.H.

Index